MW00339598

World War II Allied Nursing Services

Martin J Brayley • Illustrated by Ramiro Bujeiro

Series editor Martin Windrow

First published in Great Britain in 2002 by Osprey Publishing
Elms Court, Chapel Way, Botley, Oxford OX2 9LP, United Kingdom.
Email: **info@ospreypublishing.com**

ISBN 1 84176 185 0

Editor: Martin Windrow
Design: Alan Hamp
Index by Alan Rutter
Originated by The Electronic Page Company, Cwmbran, UK
Printed in China through World Print Ltd.

02 03 04 05 06   10 9 8 7 6 5 4 3 2 1

FOR A CATALOGUE OF ALL BOOKS PUBLISHED BY
OSPREY MILITARY AND AVIATION PLEASE CONTACT:

The Marketing Manager, Osprey Direct UK
PO Box 140, Wellingborough,
Northants, NN8 2FA, United Kingdom
Email: **info@ospreydirect.co.uk**

The Marketing Manager, Osprey Direct USA
c/o MBI Publishing, PO Box 1,
729 Prospect Ave, Osceola, WI 54020, USA
Email: **info@ospreydirectusa.com**

www.ospreypublishing.com

Author's Note

This work offers a brief introduction to female medical personnel and nursing services as part of, attached to, or auxiliary to the Allied military medical services, and responsible for the treatment, care or welfare of military casualties. As with any work of this size, it can only be considered as a primer giving a brief overview. Inevitably, the emphasis has been on British and American services; however, the experiences of the Commonwealth and other Allied nursing services are briefly described, and can generally be understood as being parallel to British and US experience. Readers are also referred to the same author's and illustrator's Men-at-Arms 357, *World War II Allied Women's Services*, which includes a good deal of material relevant to the present subject, particularly in the field of service uniforms.

Acknowledgements

New Zealand Department of Defence, Canadian War Museum, British Red Cross, Netley Hospital Museum, Ian Austin, László Békési, Philippe Charbonnier, Brian Schultz & estate of TSgt V.P.Schultz, Patrick Kirby, Tony & Joan Poucher, Alice Shepherd, Ed Storey, Martin Windrow, Simon Van Lint.

Artist's Note

Readers may care to note that the original paintings from which the colour plates in this book were prepared are available for private sale. All reproduction copyright whatsoever is retained by the Publishers. All enquiries should be addressed to:

Ramiro Bujeiro, C.C.28, 1602 Florida, Argentina

The Publishers regret that they can enter into no correspondence upon this matter.

OPPOSITE **Nurses were expected to maintain high standards of cleanliness, whatever the conditions in which they served – including tented stations close behind the front lines, often in extreme climates, with water supplies at a premium. Simply washing their clothing under field conditions was a challenge. Here, struggling to do her laundry at a General Hospital in North Africa, a collapsible canvas basin is the only means available to this British nursing sister of Queen Alexandra's Imperial Military Nursing Service (Reserve) – the British Army's principal nursing service. The 'medal' on the right breast of her lancer-fronted grey ward dress is the badge of the QAIMNS(R), worn on a dark blue suspension ribbon with two light grey outer and two red inner side-stripes. (Territorial Army nurses of the TANS wore their badge in the same position, on a scarlet ribbon with a light grey centre stripe.) Note also the broad red edges to her epaulettes, with the two bronze lieutenant's 'pips' – the equivalent rank for a nursing sister.**

WORLD WAR II ALLIED NURSING SERVICES

HISTORICAL BACKGROUND

ISTORICALLY, THE CARE AND TREATMENT of the wounded and sick during military campaigns had always been haphazard. The number of physicians and surgeons available to armies had always been absurdly small, and the crudest sort of nursing was provided, if at all, by the soldiers' women among the camp followers. As the 'age of enlightenment' dawned in the 18th century the degree of medical care differed from nation to nation, but was generally characterised by scientific ignorance and a waste of human life. Although medical and surgical advances were pioneered over the next 150 years the quality of care remained extremely patchy. The great majority of deaths were due to disease; but a high mortality rate among the wounded was inevitable, given the minimal arrangements for bringing the casualties to treatment. If they did reach the surgeons alive, many were carried off by post-operative shock or sepsis due to lack of anaesthetics, ignorance and poor hygiene.

The 18th-century Austrian army had an exceptionally well-planned medical service for its day; the dedication and foresight of Baron Larrey, chief surgeon to Napoleon's Imperial Guard, became legendary; but it was not until the Crimean War (1854–56) that nursing reforms, based on post-surgical care and hygiene, were pioneered in the British service by Florence Nightingale at her hospital at Scutari.

The Director-General of medical services, Sir Andrew Smith, was a humane and energetic man, and on paper his preparations for the campaign were admirable; but lack of resources and administrative incompetence sabotaged his plans, with calamitous consequences. The catalyst for the improvement in this, as in other fields, was William Howard Russell, the correspondent for *The Times*. At a time when journalists were beginning to provide the public with eyewitness reports that were in stark contrast to the sanitised official bulletins, Russell's despatch of 12 September 1854 was wholly damning of the British medical services. It convinced the Secretary of State at War, Sidney Herbert, that nurses were needed in the Crimea; and that the ideal person to lead them would be an old acquaintance of his, Florence Nightingale. Miss Nightingale thus became the first officially appointed British military nurse, serving with the Army but not a part of it.

The social prejudices of the day restricted the active roles of women in society; and while nursing slowly gained a general public acceptance, military nursing was slow to achieve the same recognition – war was felt to be a strictly male domain. The necessary education was open only to the upper classes, but it was considered unbecoming for a lady to lower herself to the menial tasks and rough company required of military

El Alamein, October 1942: the first link in the chain of evacuation – the Regimental Aid Post of a battalion of 51st (Highland) Division. It is simply a designated patch of sand, marked by small red cross flags amid the barbed wire in the background, where the stretcher-bearers leave the wounded. The MO is giving one man water; most of the blanket-covered casualties use their small packs as pillows; field dressings, a drink and a cigarette are about all they can hope for at this stage. (Imperial War Museum E18493)

nurses – these tasks were best left to men, and thus were all too frequently just left... . Nevertheless, the situation slowly improved, largely due to the Victorian middle-class ethos of charitable public service.

The next half-century saw constant advances in medical science and improvements in patient care, which were to reduce the heavy mortality rate from wounds and sickness – and thus to increase the rate at which men could be returned to active duty, with advantages obvious even to the least compassionate. The role of nursing in this equation was soon appreciated by all; but recognition of the need for a large and organised military nursing service was still masked by the dedicated efforts of idealistic amateurs.

The Army Nursing Service finally came into being in 1889, and had 800 trained nurses by the end of the Boer War in 1902. At this time the Royal Army Medical Corps probably led the world in its standards of medical knowledge – not only clinical, but also administrative, logistic, and across the whole related field of sanitation and hygiene. During the Boer War (1899–1902) survival rates among the wounded were far higher than a generation before. Nevertheless, although foreign observers were sufficiently impressed to urge the copying of British practice in their own armies, a subsequent royal commission found that under the burden of numbers of casualties, particularly from disease, practice had fallen short of theoretical standards. For every one of the 22,000 troops treated for wounds, 20 were hospitalised suffering from disease – some 74,000 came down with enteric and dysentery alone, and at unit level standards of hygiene were still lamentable. As a result of the commission's findings, effective reforms at all levels were driven through in 1905–10 by the Director-General, Sir Alfred Keough, and the War Secretary, Lord Haldane, and the whole chain of evacuation was reorganised.

In the United States, thousands of women came forward to tend the wounded during the Civil War (1861–65). 'Nursing' at this time largely meant providing for general welfare rather than medical care, however – bathing and feeding patients or laundering linen. Civilian volunteer nurses worked in hospitals behind the lines, provided by charitable and church organisations; actual medical care was provided by soldiers of the Confederate and Union Army medical departments, whose shortcomings were much the same as in armies the world over. Some 30 years later the Spanish-American War (1898) found the US Army Medical Department severely undermanned, and the shortage of qualified male medical orderlies led to the recruitment of female nurses qualified in medical care and graduates of civilian nursing schools or institutions. These women were not a part of the Army but were termed 'contract nurses', many being under the control of voluntary organisations rather than the Army. It was 1901 before the US Army established its own permanent military nursing service.

World War I

The unprecedented numbers of casualties suffered during the Great War (1914–18) would once and for all confirm the necessity of having fully trained nurses as a permanent part of the military medical organisation. Although the sheer numbers of casualties to be treated were overwhelming, the actual ratios of recovery reflected well on both recent advances in medical capability, and also on the practical and psychological benefits of care by qualified nursing sisters. (In 1914–18 the percentages of deaths among those who were admitted to British medical units were 7.61 per cent of the wounded and 0.91 per cent of the sick. The important distinction is that these impressive recovery figures applied only to those *who reached medical care*.) The chain of evacuation – though often delayed and distorted by the horrific local conditions – took a casualty from his Regimental Aid Post, to a Collecting Post, to Advanced and Main Dressing Stations, and a Casualty Clearing Station, before further distribution, if necessary to a large General Hospital with specialist facilities. (From the Western Front, some 40 per cent of wounded and sick were evacuated back to Great Britain.)

Under pressure of numbers and the types of multiple wounds encountered, the Casualty Clearing Station soon lost its purely 'sorting' role, and both expanded and moved forward towards the fighting line. It acquired specialist facilities and a staff of nursing sisters, and in some cases could take up to 1,000 patients. A broad generalisation would be that by 1916 the benefit had been recognised of surgical intervention earlier than had previously been thought wise; and this required the forward movement of those facilities in which nurses were stationed.

The many thousands of women who followed the vocation of nursing were thoroughly trained and usually highly efficient. At a time when women's place in society was a subject of constant debate, educated women were well aware that the professional respect of male colleagues was hard-earned, and set themselves extremely high standards. Their work in forward areas was often undertaken in unavoidably squalid conditions. No concessions were made for a nursing sister's sheltered upbringing or her youth; she was expected to face the most appalling sights and distressing responsibilities with calm competence, and was subject to strict discipline. Casualties' memoirs make clear that the great majority of nurses rose to these demands, making an unforgettable impression on those for whom they cared.

The decline of the military in the post-war era saw the reduction of the military nursing services to, in most cases, a mere handful of sisters; reliance was placed on a reserve of qualified nurses to be drawn from the civilian sector in time of need. This expectation of availability led to some strain during the early part of World War II, when Britain's cities

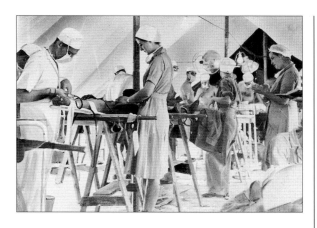

Sicily, 1943: the operating theatre in a US tented field hospital clearly illustrates the basic conditions in which operations were undertaken. Here multiple casualties are treated at the same time on litters placed on trestle tables.

Conditions for the first US Army nurses to arrive in French North Africa in winter 1942/43 were far from ideal. Tolerable in the dry season, tents were cold and muddy during the Tunisian winter; the oil stove at the rear of this tent provided little warmth. Alongside the cot on the left is a pair of 'Shoes, Nurse's, White' – which must have required great patience and effort to keep clean.

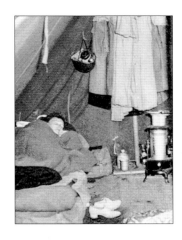

Sicily, 1943: a wounded British soldier lies on his air-portable stretcher, shaded from the sun by the tail of the air ambulance Hudson that will evacuate him to a field hospital in Tunisia. A second casualty has been lifted from an ambulance and is being assessed by a doctor before the flight.

The evacuation hospital on the Anzio beachhead was hit by enemy artillery and bombs on a number of occasions. Protection was afforded to the flimsy tents by digging shallow ditches round them and using the soil to build low splinterproof walls – see the bottom left corner of the picture.

were suffering heavily at the hands of the Luftwaffe and civilian nurses found themselves heavily burdened by huge numbers of civil casualties. The shortage of nurses was met by the Voluntary Aid Detachments, whose service to civilian and military nursing during World War II is often overlooked but was absolutely essential. The VADs were further supplemented in British service by specialist Auxiliary Territorial Service ranks; and in the United States the Women's Army Corps provided hospital aides trained in a variety of employments, as did many other organisations.

WORLD WAR II

From battlefield to base hospital

The organisation of British and US medical facilities that allowed a wounded man to be removed from the battlefield, treated and returned to a hospital was a complex system, by virtue of being a necessarily flexible one. A complicated arrangement of medical facilities, connected by alternative 'rearwards' and 'sideways' links, allowed for the most appropriate treatment of all levels of injury, from immediate stabilising care in the field, through to surgical operations and extended aftercare.

The further forward a facility was stationed, the greater the danger and strain faced by its personnel, the more urgent their need to process casualties towards the rear, and the more difficult to achieve such evacuations quickly. Regimental Aid Posts, Walking Wounded Clearing Posts and Advanced Dressing Stations were (usually) not far behind the front line, and although not deliberately targeted by German forces they often came under artillery fire and air attack through 'the fog of war'. In the Asian theatre they faced even worse perils: the Japanese regarded medical facilities and personnel as legitimate targets, and from their first victories in early 1942 they committed grisly massacres of doctors, nurses and patients in captured hospitals.

As well as keeping up with any advance, these forward links in the medical chain had to be ready to withdraw at short notice should any enemy offensive or counter-attack break the line; there were some occasions when a single unit had to pack up everything and everyone and drive off to a new location as many as three times in 24 hours.

When he was wounded in combat, an Allied casualty was expected to provide himself with immediate aid using a field dressing; where circumstances permitted he could be aided by a comrade, but all ranks knew that during an engagement pressing on with the mission took first priority, regardless of personal feelings for fallen comrades. As soon as possible the unit's stretcher-bearers (in British service normally the unit bandsmen, who would follow close behind any assault) would recover the injured man to the *Regimental Aid Post*. The bearers' medical training would generally have been only sufficient to enable them to apply immediate field dressings, their medical supplies being limited to a 'shell dressing' haversack with 15 such packets. In the US Army the 'medics' at unit level were not stretcher-bearers, and gave only immediate first aid before leaving the casualty to be found by the following litter-bearers from the divisional *Medical Battalion,* who would carry them to the *Battalion Aid Station,* equivalent to the British RAP.

Once at the RAP the unit's Medical Officer would provide emergency treatment to stabilise the injury prior to removal to the *Casualty Clearing Post,* to which 'walking wounded' would also be directed after an initial examination and labelling. Here the casualty would be collected by RAMC stretcher-bearers of the *Field Ambulance* (in the US Army, one of three *Collecting Companies*), who would transfer him the two or three miles to the brigade's *Advanced Dressing Station* (US, regimental *Collecting Station*). The ADS would classify wounded into one of three categories: (1) suffering from shock and in need of immediate aid; (2) fit to travel but requiring an immediate operation; or (3) fit to travel. Staff would then provide life-sustaining treatment such as blood transfusions, and arrange for the next move.

This, determined by wound classification, would eventually take the casualty to the divisional *Casualty Clearing Station,* which might be a few or many miles to the rear, depending on local circumstances. (US practice was to have two Clearing Stations, which alternated during the advance, leap-frogging one another to keep one team working while the other rested – both could function simultaneously if needed.) Alternatively, those too seriously wounded to survive an immediate move to the CCS (i.e. category 1 above) would be taken instead to a divisional *Field Dressing Station,* normally only a few miles away, where they would be given transfusions and treatment for shock, and cared for until sufficiently stable to be moved to the CCS. Those fit to move but requiring immediate surgery (category 2) would be sent to an *Advanced Surgical Centre* (US, *Field Hospital Platoon*) before removal to the CCS, a General Hospital, or a

Normandy, July 1944: a US Battalion Aid Station on the outskirts of St Lô. The well-identified medics all wear helmet markings, Geneva Cross armbands, and in at least one case a large red cross on the back of the field jacket. Although medical facilities were not, apparently, deliberately targeted by German forces, many memoirs describe clearly marked stretcher-bearers being hit by enemy snipers in NW Europe during 1944–45. Some of these personnel are writing wound tags – the labels that identified the treatment already given for the information of doctors further back down the chain of evacuation. Others are applying dressings; and at left back-ground, one is giving a plasma transfusion. The new ability to separate and store plasma and whole blood for transfusion in the field was one of World War II's huge advances in military medicine. The clear plasma, without red corpuscles, could be given to patients of all blood types. Depending on the wound, however, many casualties could only be kept stable for a limited time with plasma before being transfused with typed whole blood.

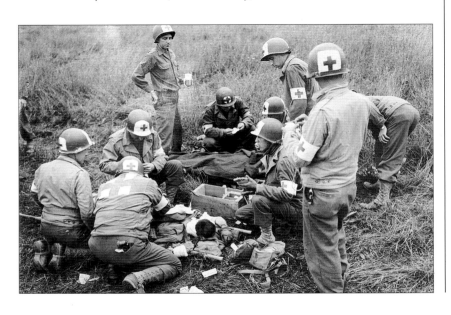

railhead. (The CCS and the ASC were normally the most 'forward' facilities where nurses were stationed, although as circumstances required they might often be found working nearer the line; they were also present at all further stages of the chain to the rear.) These small mobile surgical units included a surgeon and anaesthetist, orderlies, and enough supplies to carry out perhaps 100 operations without further support. They were supplemented by other mobile field units, e.g. blood transfusion, neuro-surgical and maxillo-facial surgical units.

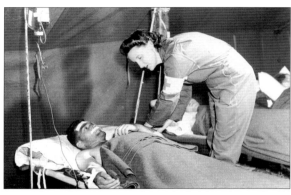

Those casualties fit to travel (category 3) would go direct to the Casualty Clearing Station. The CCS provided the patient with a high level of medical treatment and care, having operating theatres, X-ray units and all the necessary equipment for treating whatever wounds were presented. Once treated and sufficiently fit for extended travel, the patient would be moved – by motor ambulance, ambulance train, air ambulance, or river transport – to a *Forward General Hospital.* For the lightly wounded the FGH would be their last recovery area before being returned to their units. Those in need of extensive long-term care faced a stay at a *Base Hospital,* either in-theatre or overseas. This might be followed by a medical discharge, a return to light duties, or an extended stay in a *Convalescent Depot.* (US and British practices were generally similar at these later stages of the chain.)

ABOVE **The wards of tented field hospitals were quite spartan, but once casualties were sufficiently stabilised they were quickly moved back to Base Hospitals. Basic wards consisted of canvas tents furnished with field cots and the minimum of essential equipment. Here a US Army Nurse Corps sister, wearing two-piece WAC HBT fatigues ('Trousers and Shirt, Herringbone Twill, Women's, Special') checks on a GI receiving intravenous plasma.**

*   *   *

Casualty evacuation in France in 1940 was complicated by the chaotic conditions of a general retreat; casualties might take 36 hours to reach a CCS, with fatal results. Evacuation in the NW European theatre in 1944–45 was usually straightforward and distances acceptably short; a wounded man who could be reached and started back down the chain by his unit medics fairly soon after being hit had a good chance of skilled treatment within an hour or two, and consequently a high probability of recovery from even serious wounds. However, the British campaign in North Africa, 1940–42, involved extremely extended lines of communication and often fluid movement. At its severest the distance back to the RAP of, say, an armoured unit during an advance could be as much as 50 miles, with another 25 miles to the ADS. A further journey of scores of miles would eventually lead to the CCS, from where it might be hundreds of miles more to a General Hospital – a total of as many as 800 miles from the point of combat.

While the route back to base facilities was sometimes desperately long in the North African desert, at least it was practicable. In mountain terrain with few motorable roads it was a very

1943 saw the repatriation of many British POWs formerly held in Italy; here the hospital ship *Newfoundland* arrives at a West Country port to be greeted by a group of Red Cross volunteers. Hospital ships, introduced by the British for the Boer War in South Africa (1899–1902), were vital for the long-range mass transportation of wounded; well equipped for patient care, they carried a full complement of medical and nursing staff.

OPPOSITE **Basic fieldcraft became a standard element of US Army Nurse Corps training; all nurses were instructed in digging foxholes, combat survival and field hygiene. This smiling pair are obviously enjoying their stint playing soldiers at Fort Lewis, Washington, and have been issued male clothing and equipment to make the training a little more bearable; both wear the 'Mackinaw' and HBT fatigues, and carry the M1943 folding e-tool, M1936 musette and service respirator.**

different story. The mountain battlefields of Italy in the winters of 1943 and 1944 were often inaccessible to anything but hand-carried stretchers and pack mules; before even a jeep rigged for carrying stretcher cases could reach him, an infantryman's first stage down the chain of evacuation might be an agonising, jolting journey down muddy rock slopes during which progress was measured in hours per mile rather than miles per hour.

The same was true in the Far East, particularly during such campaigns as the British 'Chindit' operations behind enemy lines in Burma, and the Australian operations in New Guinea. Here the jungle, swamp and mountain terrain – especially in the wet season – made the normal evacuation procedures impossible. For many casualties the horrendous journey from the place of wounding to even an Advanced Dressing Station was the worst phase of the ordeal; on one occasion in the Arakan campaign on the Burmese coast in late 1942 it took six stretcher-bearers more than 17 hours to take one stretcher case and two 'walking wounded' from an RAP to an ADS just three miles away. To get back to a CCS the casualty might then face being driven perhaps 50 miles in an ambulance over the most primitive roads imaginable. Alternatively, in confined positional fighting like the battle of Kohima, evacuation was impossible and unit MOs had to care for the wounded as best they could while under fire – and the threat of barbarous massacre if the Japanese broke through.

If he was lucky, the casualty's long overland journey might lead him to a jungle airstrip. Although medical facilities in the field were limited, at least by 1944 the introduction of rapid air evacuation enabled those wounded who lived long enough to see the inside of a Dakota to be sent straight to a major base hospital complex after a matter of less than two hours in the air. Before increased US resources allowed air evacuation, such a journey was often unsurvivable; in Burma in 1942 it had sometimes taken six weeks to carry a man back to a General Hospital by conventional means.

Despite the strong element of luck involved in an individual casualty's progress down the first stages of the chain of evacuation, in general the Western medical services during World War II were remarkably successful. Recent advances both in clinical techniques and pharmacology obviously played a huge part. The wide availability from 1943 of penicillin and sulphonamide drugs greatly reduced the risks of local and systemic septicaemia; and the ability to store whole blood and plasma for transfusion saved countless lives. Allied to these, however, the well thought-out chain of evacuation, and the excellent nursing care which was tirelessly provided at many stages of that process, made a major contribution. Overall, 94 per cent of the British casualties who reached a Casualty Clearing Station would survive, and a similar proportion of US casualties – figures that could not have been dreamt of in previous wars.

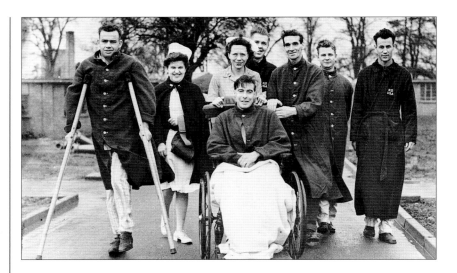

Wounded GIs, recuperating in England, take the air with two US Army Nurse Corps nurses. The nurse at left wears the white ward dress with red-lined dark blue cape; her companion wears the blue ward dress. Two of the patients – e.g. far right – wear US Army Medical Department dressing gowns, the rest wear the British 'hospital blues' gown.

GREAT BRITAIN

Queen Alexandra's Royal Naval Nursing Service

The year 1884 saw the first authorised use of female naval nurses, receiving royal sanction in 1902 when they became the QARNNS under the patronage of King Edward VII's popular Danish-born consort. Although given the privileges of officer rank, naval nurses were civilians and had no military status. At the outbreak of war in September 1939 there were 90 Regular QARNNS sisters, a figure that would remain relatively constant – 99 in 1940, 98 in 1941, 94 in 1942, 88 in 1943, 86 in 1944, and 87 in 1945. The numbers of **QARNNS (Reserve)** nurses were to rise quite rapidly, however, approximate annual numbers being 218 in 1940, 250 in 1941, 318 in 1942, 600 in 1943, 636 in 1944, and reaching a peak of 971 in 1945.

QARNNS sisters were often required to serve abroad; at the outbreak of the war there were RN Hospitals in Malta and Hong Kong, and these were soon supplemented by a number of newly established sick quarters as well as auxiliary and military hospitals around the world, from Durban to Trincomalee. Nurses were also to serve aboard some of the 11 hospital ships: HMHS *Amarapoora, Cap St Jaques, Empire Clyde, Gerusalemme, Isle of Jersey, Maine, Ophir, Oxfordshire, Tjitjalengka, Vasna* and *Vita*. No awards for gallantry were made to QARNNS personnel during World War II, although many sisters did find themselves 'at the sharp end' – one spent five days in an open liferaft following the sinking of the ship on which she was in transit.

Uniforms The distinctive ward dress of the QARNNS (see Plate A1) was designed by their patron, Queen Alexandra, and did not change in essentials apart from evolving fashions of length and cut. It consisted of a dark blue button-front dress, detachable white collar and red cuffs, white apron, and white veil bearing on the rear the naval crown in dark blue. A blue tippet or cape bore narrow red piping outlining an inner border for ranks of Nursing Sister and Senior Nursing Sister, and a broad solid red border for Superintending Sister and above. On the right breast of the tippet was displayed an embroidered badge in gold, white and red on a black rectangular patch. Tropical uniform consisted of a white cotton dress with full-length button front, white tippet with red trim, and a white 'trilby' style hat for formal wear. A blue fabric belt was worn with the temperate uniform and a white one with the tropical dress, though period images suggest that the white belt was often used with the temperate uniform; the round silver clasp plate bore a crown over a fouled anchor within a wreath.

In 1942 an 'outdoor' uniform was issued; this was based on the Women's Royal Naval Service officer's uniform of a navy blue double-breasted jacket and skirt, but differed in having rank worn as epaulettes rather than as cuff rings, and a cap badge based on the QARNNS crown, anchor and monogram on a black backing patch (as also worn on the white tropical trilby).

In April 1945 the little-known **Royal Naval Medical Air Evacuation Unit** was formed in the Far East in an effort to ensure rapid removal of wounded from the tropical environment, which hindered recovery. A total of 12 nurses were trained, in two successive classes of six. Naval air evacuation nurses initially wore a uniform consisting of Australian khaki drill (KD) tunic and slacks with a bush hat; this was later replaced by a purpose-made khaki uniform with RN buttons, QARNNS badges on the epaulettes, and a navy blue cap. A specialisation badge consisting of a half-wing bearing the letters 'RNMAEU' was worn by all air evacuation nurses; this short run of badges was locally produced using the skills of a naval dentist!

QARNNS and WRNS relative ranks

QARNNS	WRNS
Matron-in-Chief	Commandant
Principal Matron	Superintendent
Matron	Chief Officer
Superintending Sister	First Officer
Senior Nursing Sister	Second Officer
Nursing Sister	Third Officer

Female medical officers, RNVR

Only 21 female medical officers served with the medical branch of the Royal Navy during the war, as members of the Royal Naval Volunteer Reserve. These doctors were not recruited specifically to undertake the care of WRNS ranks but of all members of the service. Their employment was generally centred on large port areas and naval hospitals. Uniform was as for WRNS officers, but with RNVR medical branch lieutenant's or lieutenant-commander's cuff rank, and gold embroidered officer's cap badge (see Plate A2). The first female medical officer, Medical Superintendent Dr.G.Rewcastle, had been a member of the WRNS but was transferred to the RNVR in the rank of surgeon lieutenant, after which all subsequent female MOs joined the RNVR with naval rank.

Queen Alexandra's Imperial Military Nursing Service
Territorial Army Nursing Service

The Army Nursing Service came into being in 1889. By the end of the Boer War in 1902 the ANS had 800 trained nurses, and their sterling service in that conflict led to royal recognition and improved status, with a change of title to QAIMNS. The **QAIMNS (Reserve)** was formed just prior to World War I in anticipation of an increased demand on the medical services. In 1914 there were around 300 Reserves; by the end of the Great War that number exceeded 10,000, with another 8,495 nurses serving with the military being provided by civilian organisations such as the Red Cross and the Order of St John.

Royal Naval Sick Quarters, Stornoway, 1943, showing the mixture of uniforms worn by the female staff: left foreground, a QARNNS(R) sister (cf Plate A1); a group of VADs in blue ward dress with white apron – note, left background, the brassard with 'Mobile' badge; centre background, a VAD wearing the dark blue 'outdoor' uniform; and right foreground, a QARNNS Superintending Sister.

Each separate branch of the British Army nursing service had its own distinctive insignia which were worn on the cap and collar of 'outdoor' uniforms. TOP **The insignia of the QAIMNS was a silver cross of Dannebrog within a gilt oval garter bearing the service title and surmounted by a crown, the whole above a scroll bearing the motto SUB CRUCE CANDIDA ('Under the sign of the white cross'). The insignia of the QAINMNS(R) is illustrated on Plate A.** ABOVE **The TANS insignia resembled that of the QAIMNS but was all in silver, with the entwined 'AA' monogram of Queen Alexandra, the service title and a scroll bearing FORTITUDO MEA DEUS ('God is my strength').**

In September 1939 the QAIMNS had fewer than 700 Regular nurses, but apart from mobilisation of the Reserve the Army nursing service was further supplemented by the members of the **Territorial Army Nursing Service**; the TANS was merged administratively with the QAIMNS for the duration of the war (although TANS badges continued to be worn). All QAIMNS nurses were afforded officer status, wearing relative (but non-equivalent) rank badges from 1940. Prior to the award of Army rank insignia a nurse's rank had been shown by scarlet braid at the cuff of the ward dress. In 1941 all Army nurses were granted commissions and awarded equivalent Army ranks. In mixed units they were to salute and were saluted as per regulations. During World War II the 'QAs' served world-wide in locations from China, India and Burma, to Egypt, Sudan and Malta. During the war the Army nursing services suffered 190 deaths in service, of which 26 were QAIMNS ranks, 134 QAIMNS(R) and 30 TANS.

Upon application for service all prospective members of the nursing services were required to be already qualified and practising with at least (in Great Britain) State Registered Nurse status. Although there were minor differences in conditions of acceptance between the services, in general all required the same high degree of mental and physical ability, along with highly developed personal skills and standards of behaviour. For the British these qualities also had to include being a British subject (of European descent), no older than 35, single or widowed and without children. Personal appearance was a contributory factor in selection, e.g. serious scarring or bad teeth counted against applicants.

'MEDICAL EXAMINATION OF CANDIDATES FOR ADMISSION TO QUEEN ALEXANDRA'S IMPERIAL MILITARY NURSING SERVICE (Ref. para. 487.)
INSTRUCTIONS FOR MEDICAL BOARDS
1. The boards must bear in mind that these ladies are called on to serve not only at home but in many foreign stations with trying climates, and the medical examination must therefore be thoroughly carried out.
2. The vision should be sufficient for ordinary purposes, but squint or any other morbid condition of the eyes will cause the rejection of the candidate.
3. Particular attention will be paid to the following points:-
(a) That the candidate's hearing is good.
(b) That she has no impediment in her speech.
(c) That her teeth are in good order; decayed teeth, if well filled, will be considered as sound. Loss of teeth up to a reasonable extent will not cause rejection, provided that in the opinion of the board the candidate is fitted with efficient dentures which enable her to masticate her food properly.
(d) The heart and lungs are healthy.
(e) That she does not suffer from varicose veins to an extent that would interfere with the efficient performance of her duties.
(f) That she has no congenital malformation or defect.
(g) That she has no chronic skin disease.
4. Candidates will be required to furnish particulars of any serious injury or illness from which they have previously suffered.
5. Candidates will also be asked if they are ruptured or if they have ever had fits.

6. The general appearance of candidates, especially with reference to anaemia, will be noted.

7. In the event of rejection, the cause will be clearly stated in the proceedings of the board.' (From *Regulations for the Medical Services of the Army*, 1938)

Uniforms Traditionally nurses had worn a grey uniform dress with white veil bearing the service insignia; this was worn with a tippet in red for Regular nurses or grey with red trim for Reserves – TANS wore the grey tippet with red trim but with the addition of a pair of gilt 'Ts' at the corners. A corridor cape was worn in inclement weather; in length this was to reach the finger tips when the arms were straight at the sides, but in practice it provided little warmth. Although the grey ward dress was used in most theatres of war, a smart white tropical dress was also available, but this tended to be kept for 'walking-out' uniform.

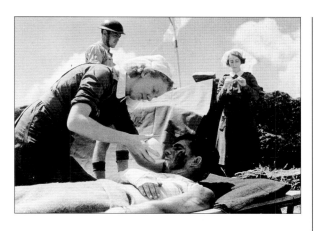

A posed photograph showing nurses working at an Advanced Dressing Station during operations in Sicily, August 1943. The two QAIMNS sisters (identified by their medal-like breast 'badge' and epaulettes) wear the early style lancer-fronted ward dress with long sleeves and white collar – an item not best suited to active service.

Three basic variants of the grey dress were used during the war: a lancer-front pattern; a straight-front fly pattern; and the 'field force' dress with front fly and detachable sleeves (see Plate B3). The provision for rank epaulettes to be worn on the shoulder enabled the ward dress to be worn without the tippet (which also bore epaulettes); these were red for QAIMNS and grey with broad red edge trim for QAIMNS(R) and TANS.

For off-duty and formal dress a grey barathea uniform was worn in the distinctive 'Norfolk' cut, with a button-front belt (see Plate B1). The original trilby-type hat was replaced in 1943 by a pattern identical to that worn by the ATS. The grey fabric of the Norfolk-cut uniform proved to be difficult to obtain during the war, and from January 1944 nurses were ordered to wear khaki Service Dress as worn by ATS officers, with the appropriate nursing service collar and cap badges, and a double lanyard in red and light grey on the right shoulder. A khaki ATS pattern greatcoat was also authorised for use during the winter months.

The campaign in North Africa showed the ward dress to be, at best, unsuited to field use, and male pattern Battledress was issued. A limited number of ATS items were also used, but procurement limitations left most nurses wearing poorly fitting male clothing. The invasion of Europe in June 1944 found nurses similarly poorly equipped for field work; once again male pattern BD was widely issued, along with 37 Pattern web equipment with brace extensions in lieu of ammunition pouches, respirators, messtins and steel helmets (see Plate B2).

For tropical use nurses initially wore a white dress and a white felt trilby; this was later replaced by KD bush shirts, slacks and 'spats' shaped like US web leggings, all of which were theoretically impervious to penetration by mosquitoes. Like the field force dress, the KD 'Shirt, Mosquito, Nursing Officers' had button-on detachable long sleeves, providing a cooler garment during the heat of the day but allowing for

France, summer 1944: a sister of the Territorial Army Nursing Service wearing a 'Cap, GS' with the TANS badge; a 'Blouse, Battledress, Serge, ATS' adorned with the ribbon of the 1939–43 (later 1939–45) Star; Service Dress skirt (economically lengthened by the addition of a short length of material to the hem); and carrying a tan raincoat. She seems to have the Lightweight Respirator and a steel helmet slung behind her right hip.

cover in the evenings. Despite the issue of BD and KD uniforms the grey ward dress was still frequently used, even in the jungle hospitals of Burma.

QAIMNS and Army relative ranks

QAIMNS	Army
Matron-in-Chief	Brigadier
Chief Principal Matron*	Colonel
Principal Matron	Lieutenant-Colonel
Matron	Major
Senior Sister (10 years' service)	Captain
Sister	Lieutenant

* Prior to the award of the King's Commission in 1941 the rank of Chief Principal Matron did not exist, the Matron-in-Chief being equivalent to colonel. The position of Staff Nurse which, with Sister, ranked as lieutenant, was discontinued at this time.

Most of the Commonwealth nursing services used dresses of designs similar to those in use with the British services.

Female officers, Royal Army Medical Corps

During the war, 150 female doctors served with the RAMC with equal rank and status to male doctors. Candidates had to be qualified as doctors prior to joining, and once accepted for service they attended a four-week basic training course to introduce them to Army life and routines before being sent on their first postings. Upon commissioning, doctors held the rank of lieutenant, with automatic promotion to captain following 12 months' satisfactory service; specialists could hold the rank of major. While a number of medical posts were open to female MOs the majority were employed in the care of ATS personnel in a general practitioner role, at training and mixed AA units, or as district MOs.

Female medical officers wore ATS officer's uniform with RAMC buttons and collar badges; the ATS cap with RAMC badge, or RAMC coloured Field Service cap (see Plate C1). As members of the RAMC female doctors were allowed to wear a Sam Browne belt with – unlike ATS officers – the cross strap.

Princess Mary's Royal Air Force Nursing Service

The youngest of the British nursing services was formed in June 1918 as the RAF Nursing Service, to support the newly unified RAF in a role previously undertaken by Army nurses – a number of whom transferred to the new service. The following year service numbers had reached 130, but post-war economies prevented progress with the service structure other than changing the title to Princes Mary's Royal Air Force Nursing Service in 1923.

At the outbreak of war in 1939, PMRAFNS sisters were serving at RAF Hospitals Ely, Wroughton, and Halton, and overseas in Palestine, Aden and Iraq as well as in smaller station sick quarters. By the end of the war 'PMs' were serving in every theatre of operations including NW Europe

Burma, spring 1944: located in a former Chin native shack, a forward ambulance unit provides temporary shelter and care for soldiers of the 5th Indian Infantry Division wounded in the fighting for Tiddim during the Japanese Kohima/Imphal offensive. The QAIMNS(R) sister wears the grey 'Dress, Field Force, Nursing Officers' – see Plate B3.

and Burma. Those seeking a career in the PMRAFNS had to have recognised civil qualifications as State Registered Nurses; to have served for at least four years in a nursing role; and to be between the ages of 22 and 45 (although the age limits were relaxed during the war to aid recruitment). Like the other women's services, the PMRAFNS legally became full members of the armed forces in 1941. Before March 1943 PMs held officer status but not rank; after this date they were accorded commissions in the RAF with equivalent rank badges, under AMO A196. Previously rank 'appointment' had been shown by light blue cuff stripes on maroon backing for Senior Sisters and Matrons and light blue on dark blue for Sisters; after this date RAF-style light blue on dark blue lace was used to identify their RAF ranks. However, as in all the military nursing services, it was still customary for the nurses to be addressed by their nursing title rather than by their military rank.

Uniforms The summer service uniform of the PMRAFNS consisted of a fine barathea tunic and skirt in RAF blue-grey. The tunic was of the typical nursing service 'Norfolk' cut, with a three-button front and buttoned waistbelt and a flapped pocket at each hip (see Plate C2). The six-gore skirt was worn longer than normal wartime fashion, to within ten inches of the ground. With this uniform were worn two different hats. For formal dress headgear was a black felt four-cornered hat, similar to the tricorn worn by the WRNS but with an extra corner at rear centre of the brim. For less formal duties a 'storm cap' was worn: this resembled a smaller-crowned version of the WAAF cap but without a visor, and with the badge worn on a turned-up flap at the front. (This style was also used by VADs early in the war.) During the winter months an RAF blue-grey barathea dress was worn, with a matching tippet and a white veil bearing the RAF wings in dark blue at centre rear. A blue-grey 'corridor cape' was also issued, as well as an RAF-style greatcoat.

For field service the PMs were granted the concession of the issue of a WAAF 'work suit' (i.e Battledress) blouse. No matching trousers were officially issued, entailing the odd mix of work blouse with service dress skirt. Ward dress was based on the universal white nursing dress with full-length button front and hip pockets. A white veil, stockings and shoes were worn with the ward dress. With all forms of dress the RAF caduceus badge was worn on collar points or a corresponding position.

The PMRAFNS 'storm cap' in RAF blue-grey with a black ribbed band, and turn-up flaps at front and rear. It is being worn here in Belgium in January 1945 in conjunction with the WAAF 'working suit' blouse of field uniform, although a blue-grey beret was authorised for field use. It bears the RAF officer's full-colour embroidered cap badge; and note RAF rank lace equivalent to flying officer on the epaulette. This shape of cap was also worn by VADs – see Plate A3; one former VAD describes them as 'terrible little navy blue hats known as "egg cups"'. (IWM CL2406)

Two PMRAFNS sisters wearing white ward dress with the blue-grey tippet. This is adorned with the RAF medical service caduceus, and shoulder boards showing rank as adopted in March 1943 under AMO A196, which awarded PMs commissions in the RAF with equivalent rank badges.

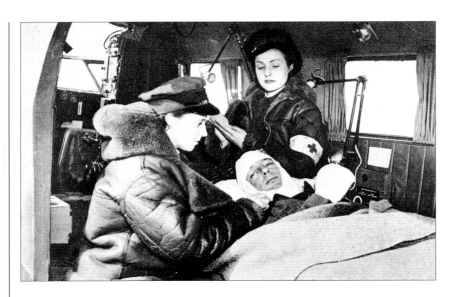

The PMRAFNS was supplemented by **WAAF Nursing Orderlies** and members of the VAD. A small number of these women were trained in air evacuation but, unlike the RNMAEU and the US ANC flight nurses, they were not required to be qualified nurses. WAAF Nursing Orderlies wore the standard WAAF blue-grey uniforms, including the Battledress-style work blouse and slacks. For air evacuation duties they were issued partial male flying clothing, normally limited to boots, Irvin jacket, Mae West and parachute (see Plate C3).

Two WAAF flying nursing orderlies attend to an injured airman in an air evacuation aircraft. They wear the 'Suit, Working, Serge, WAAF' and WAAF service caps, with hooded Coastal Command pattern Irvin flying jackets and, no doubt, 1940 pattern flying boots.

PMRAFNS and RAF relative ranks

PMRAFNS	RAF
Matron-in-Chief	Air Commodore
Principal Matron	Wing Commander
Matron	Squadron Leader
Senior Sister	Flight Lieutenant
Sister	Flying Officer
Staff Nurse (abolished 1/4/41)	Pilot Officer

Female medical officers, Royal Air Force

The first female medical officers were appointed in 1940; as in the other women's services, RAF female MOs held relative rank until 1942, when they received commissions in the RAF. Upon appointment to the RAF medical service the rank of flying officer was normally awarded, with promotion after 12 months to the rank of flight lieutenant. Further promotion was limited and dependent upon appointment to specific senior posts, although some medical specialists joined the service with immediate appointment to higher ranks commensurate with their professional status in civilian medicine. The uniform of RAF female medical officers was as for WAAF officers but with the RAF medical branch winged caduceus badge worn on the collar points.

Voluntary Aid Detachments

The importance of the Voluntary Aid Detachments to the smooth functioning of the military medical services in time of war cannot be overstated. The initial intake of VADs were drawn from members of the Red Cross Society, St John's Ambulance Brigade and St Andrew's Ambulance Association. During World War II over 4,000 VADs served with the Royal Navy, 800 of them in overseas posts; 4,028 were employed with the Army, and 413 served with the RAF. VADs were enrolled in two

British Red Cross Society badge as worn on a VAD 'storm cap' – cf Plate A3, and portrait of Honor Fortune. The red cross on a white enamel shield is set against a gilt garter and scroll.

Hampshire VAD Honor Fortune served at RNH Haslar during the war; here she wears the British Red Cross Society dark blue 'outdoor' uniform with visored cap, the blue band with white trim. On each epaulette are brass titles: 'G1' shows that she has the BRC Grade 1 qualification; curved titles 'RED CROSS' and 'HAMPSHIRE' enclose a detachment numeral. On the left forearm is the 'MOBILE' badge (see Plate A); and below it a red 2¹/₂in bar denotes one year's war service. Service with the Royal Navy is indicated by the red badge on the upper left sleeve, 'RNH' over an anchor within a circle.

BELOW October 1939: posed group in a hospital train kept at Goodmayes, Essex, to pick up casualties shipped from France and move them to inland hospitals. Stretchers were stacked along the carriages like bunks; there was a small dressing station but no catering facilities, and the nurses were billeted on private homes locally. The train was staffed by VADs, with a civilian doctor (who gave them such training as he could), one fully qualified nurse (here in white ward dress), and St John's Ambulance Brigade volunteers as stretcher-bearers. (Courtesy Alice Shepherd)

classes, Mobile or Immobile: the former were available to serve world-wide, and the latter only within easy reach of their homes. By the end of the war well over 8,000 VADs were in service with the armed forces.

VADs could enrol into various basic and qualified categories. The basic non-qualified categories were Nursing Members, Cooks and Clerks; those with professional qualifications could be enrolled as Pharmacists, Dispensers, Radiographers, Hospital Cooks, Masseuses, Laboratory Assistants and Opticians.

Uniforms VAD members wore the uniform of their parent organisation with insignia to identify the service to which they were attached for duty. For naval appointments the insignia consisted of an anchor within a circle with the letters 'RNH' (Royal Naval Hospital) all in red, worn on the upper left sleeve. For Army appointments an RAMC cap badge was worn on the left breast; and a gilt RAF medical branch winged caduceus was worn on the collar points by those attached to the RAF medical services. A Mobile or Immobile badge was worn on the lower left sleeve of the service uniform, or on an armband when in ward dress.

Service uniform consisted of a dark blue gabardine three-button tunic, skirt and cap with white shirt and black tie. A navy blue overcoat was also issued, as was a red-lined navy blue corridor cape for use with ward dress. The headgear was initially a matching 'storm cap' resembling that of the PMRAFNS (see Plate A3); this was later replaced by a visored cap resembling the ATS type. Ward dress was a light blue-grey cotton dress with white apron and veil; a red Geneva, St John's or St Andrew's cross was displayed on the breast section of the apron and the front of the veil. Rank

The VAD ward dress: light blue-grey cotton, with separate starched white collar and cuffs, white apron and veil; a navy blue belt was worn when the apron was laid aside. The gathering of the veil behind the head was unique to the VADs; to put it on, a former VAD recalls that she pressed her forehead against a wall while gathering and pinning the material behind the neck. If lifted off carefully, the arrangement would last for days. (Courtesy Alice Shepherd)

on ward dress was signified by horizontal tapes worn on the upper sleeve. Unlike the military nursing services, the VAD veil was gathered behind the head and not bloused in the military fashion. The universal pattern white nurse's dress was worn on tropical service with veil and 'Mobile' brassard. Khaki Battledress and KD uniforms were also issued as required, as were a small number of dark blue BD uniforms.

UNITED STATES

Army Nurse Corps
On 2 February 1901 the Army Reorganisation Act (31 Stat.753) was passed by the United States Congress, making the Nurse Corps (Female) a permanent Corps of the US Army Medical Department. The Nurse Corps saw considerable enlargement during the Great War; over 12,000 nurses were serving in the spring of 1918, 5,350 of them outside the continental USA, and the Corps reached a peak strength of 21,480 by the Armistice – by which time 198 nurses had died in service. The Army Reorganisation Act 1918 (40 Stat.879) of 9 July changed the name to the Army Nurse Corps. The USA held its nurses in high regard; a career in nursing was always respected and considered a fitting contribution to the nation's war effort (which was not the case with other servicewomen, in the early days of the WAAC). In 1940 there were 1,600 Regular nurses in American military service; by 1944 this figure had risen to over 40,000, and a significant number had already given their lives in the early stages of the Pacific War – 104 ANC and NNC nurses died at Japanese hands, for instance during the brutal Bataan 'death march' of April 1942.

The latter half of 1944 saw a shortage of military nurses as the multi-theatre commitment put a strain on available numbers. Despite the fact that over 9,000 African-American nurses were registered in the USA, few were considered for military service. The Army eventually enrolled a little over 300, who were used mainly to nurse black troops and POWs.

On 22 December 1942, Public Law 828 of the 77th Congress authorised relative rank for ANC officers, from second lieutenant through to lieutenant-colonel. In June 1944 Public Law 350 of the 78th Congress granted temporary commissions to nurses of the ANC, allowing for the full pay and privileges of the rank held. The grant was applicable only for the duration of the war plus six months; it was only on 16 April 1947 that Public Law 36 of the 80th Congress made ANC commissions permanent.

Applicants for the ANC were required to be high school graduates who had undertaken an academic course of at least four years; to have further graduated from a recognised nursing school having a minimum three-year course; to be Registered Nurses; and to be married or single US citizens or citizens of Allied or co-belligerent nations. Regular nurses were accepted between the ages of 22 and 30, and Reserves from 21 to 40.

Uniforms In 1920 a khaki uniform, with a tunic styled upon that worn by male officers, was introduced for the ANC; this was still the prescribed outdoor dress in 1940 but was seldom seen – nurses rarely purchased them, finding them unattractive. The increasing number of nurses in service and the prospect of a global war led to a review of nursing uniforms in 1940. It was proposed that a two-tone blue uniform be adopted for 'outdoor' (i.e. service dress) wear, with the ubiquitous white ward uniform being retained for hospital use, along with a cape in the same blue as the new tunic. The new wool uniform had a dark blue tunic, cap and overcoat, white or blue shirt, black tie, and black shoes. The skirt was of a medium blue shade, and grey-blue suede gloves completed the uniform. The tunic had two internal skirt pockets with buttoned flaps, three front buttons and a buttoned waist belt (later deleted). The epaulettes were piped, and the cuffs trimmed, in Medical Corps maroon. The cap had an oversize visor and bloused top with a frontal bow; general dissatisfaction with this style led to the adoption of an overseas or garrison cap (sidecap) in dark blue with maroon piping (see Plate D1).

At this time uniform issue for nurses was – theoretically – one blue uniform and six white hospital dresses, with further upkeep being at the owner's rather than government expense. Non-combatant clothing enjoyed very low priority, and increased recruitment and consequent pressure on uniform procurement meant that these uniforms were initially in very short supply, with many nurses unable to obtain the complete blue uniform or full issue of hospital dresses as late as the summer of 1942. Nurses deployed to the North African theatre in 1943 found themselves expected to operate in field conditions with only their Class A blues or blue overseas hospital dress, neither of which was at all suited to living under canvas or to the extremes of terrain and climate. Wholly inadequate and vastly oversized male herringbone twill fatigues (HBTs) and boots were issued, much to the amusement of many a GI and to the chagrin of the nurses.

Further problems were encountered. The original tunic patterns made up by the Quartermaster branch had been based on male sizes and cut; even the skirt was unsuited to the female form, being too wide in the waist and too narrow in the hips. The range of sizing was also inadequate for the variety of female figures, being limited to sizes 30in.–48in. in a short, medium or long fit. The problems of size and poor cut were not rectified until 1943, when the Office of the Quartermaster General

ABOVE **The two-tone 'blues' or 'Class A' uniform ('Coat, Wool, Covert, Blue, Nurse's' and 'Skirt, Wool, Covert, Blue, Nurse's') adopted by the ANC in 1942 – cf Plate D1. It is worn here with 'Shoes, Nurse's, Black', light blue dress gloves, and the disliked 'Cap, Service, Covert, Blue, Nurse's' with frontal bow.**

LEFT **ANC nurses newly arrived in the ETO. Dressed in the 'Overcoat, Field, Women, Officer's' with M1 helmets, they are burdened with the 'Bag, Canvas, Field, OD, M1936' (musette), a bedding roll, a 'utility bag' (handbag), and three C-ration boxes providing meals for 24 hours.**

finally accepted that civilian specialists in the production of female attire were best consulted over the future procurement and specifications of ANC and WAAC uniforms.

September 1942 saw a major review of ANC uniform requirements, including procurement of Arctic, tropical and temperate clothing better suited to field use than the available blues or whites. It was also suggested that olive drab should replace the blue uniform, as being more appropriate for the intended role. The requested OD uniform was authorised initially only for those proceeding overseas, with the intention of changing US-based nurses into OD as soon as practicable but for them to retain the blues in the interim. The implementation date for the change to OD for US-based nurses was postponed a number of times, but it was finally authorised as immediate priority in December 1943, with the expectation that it would be fully implemented by June 1944 (see Plate E1). Those in possession of blues were allowed to retain them as a dress uniform, and those wishing to acquire 'dress blues' could do so at their own expense.

Moves were also made to replace the hospital whites and the blue crepe hospital dress worn when serving overseas. It was proposed that a brown and white seersucker 'wrap-over' be issued for use overseas, and perhaps eventually in all hospitals. Seersucker was not the choice of the nurses, as blue and white seersucker was then worn by trainees, who could only wear the distinctive white nurse's dress after graduation. This objection was overruled, and the seersucker wrap-over with matching 'nurse cap' was introduced for overseas service; from mid-1944 its use was authorised in the continental USA. (An early white cotton version of the seersucker with long or short sleeves, which was meant to replace the hospital dress, was found to be unsuitable and was soon discarded.) A hip-length jacket accompanied the seersucker dress, allowing for use when off duty or off the ward. In August 1943 seersucker slacks and shirt were introduced for use when the dress was deemed inappropriate, such as when tending litter (stretcher) casualties.

Unlike the WAC, the ANC was authorised issue of the male blouson-type 'M1941' field jacket. The subsequent development of the WAC field uniform based on the male 1943 pattern provided an ideal uniform for nurses in the field, and it was issued to the ANC in some quantity.

Army Air Force nurses

Although a part of the Army the USAAF had its own command structure and identity, to all intents and purposes separate from that of the ground troops. All ANC nurses assigned to duty with the AAF were required to undergo four weeks of 'acquaintance training' to introduce them to the ways of the Air Force prior to being sent to one of 238 hospitals, 375 infirmaries, 150 dispensaries or eight convalescent centres within the continental US (1944 figures), or to one of the many overseas units.

Of the total of some 6,500 ANC nurses serving with the Army Air Forces in 1944, 500 were trained as specialist **Flight Nurses**. To be eligible to apply for this duty the ANC nurse had first to have served for at least six months in an AAF hospital and to have been recommended for flight training. Provisional acceptance was followed by a full aircrew medical and fitness test; successful candidates were sent to the School of Air Evacuation at Bowman Field, Kentucky. At Bowman they spent

This image was produced for the official launch of the new ANC brown/white striped seersucker uniform; the nurse wears the 'Jacket, Cotton, Seersucker, Nurse's' over the wrap-around 'Uniform, Cotton, Seersucker, Nurse's'. A matching shirt, slacks and cap were also provided. The somewhat patronising 1943 caption reads: 'New uniform for the Army Nurse Corps... The seersucker field uniform has a companion jacket, smartly designed, which makes the nurse ready for a walk down the village street when she comes off duty. With the uniform cap, brown envelope handbag and shoes she is ready for shopping and strolling'.

eight weeks in academic, professional and military study, including emergency medical treatment, tropical medicine, and basic military fieldcraft.

Although it was against the Geneva Conventions, the nurses were taught the use of sidearms; it was considered that in some areas of operations where the nurses would find themselves the carriage of a pistol for self and patient protection would be necessary. (The Japanese did not recognise the Conventions, and the first weeks of the Asian war had shown that Allied nurses and doctors could expect absolutely no protection from their non-combatant status, before or after capture.) Most of the nurses flying the 'Hump'

ABOVE **The co-ordination programme of WAC and ANC clothing saw nurses issued with the WAC HBT uniform and the 'Waist, Wool, Women's' or 'shirtwaist'. As worn by ANC nurses this was adorned with the rank device on the right collar point and the caduceus-and-'N' on the left.**

ABOVE LEFT **USA, January 1944: the new OD winter service dress is officially launched for Stateside ANC nurses, having previously been authorised only for overseas use. A similar uniform in a lighter tropical worsted fabric was produced for summer wear. Alongside the OD uniform (left) is the old two-tone 'blues' that it would replace.**

(the China-Burma-India air route) or elsewhere in the Far East were issued with or had access to a .45in. calibre sidearm; anecdotal evidence suggests that these were made ready on some occasions, although no shots were fired in anger.

The first class arrived at Bowman in late 1942, graduating in February 1943. At that time they had no special uniform and no flight wing distinction; the addressing officer on graduation day therefore presented his own wings to the top nurse in the class, pending the official introduction of Flight Nurse wings. When these became available the newly graduated nurse was allowed to wear them on the left breast of the uniform and to draw an extra $60.00 per month while on flying duties (ANC pay was the same as for the equivalent ranks of Army officers, with e.g. a captain earning $2,400 per annum in 1944). By the end of 1943 ANC Flight Nurses were serving in all theatres of operations where AAF units were operating. On 17 January 1943 2nd Lt.Elsie Ott became the first nurse to receive the Air Medal, for nursing five patients on an 11,000-mile flight from India to the continental USA – the first international air evacuation flight in US history. (For uniform details, see Plate D2.)

Navy Nurse Corps

The NNC traced its origins to 1908, when Congress authorised a Nursing Unit of the USN Medical Corps. On 7 December 1941 the NNC had a total of 828 nurses on active duty with a further 940 reservists. Although they enjoyed officer status, relative rank was not authorised until July

Although the garrison (overseas) cap was popular its availability was limited during late 1943 and early 1944. Many ANC nurses wore the more formal 'Cap, Service, Wool, Nurse's', as in this portrait of a lieutenant in her winter service dress uniform of 'chocolate' OD fabric. On the collars all nurses, being officers, displayed pairs of the national 'U.S.' and ANC caduceus devices (see Plate E1).

Normandy, July 1944: nurses take time out for a meal eaten from messtins in the open alongside the tented accommodation and wards of their field hospital. All wear the jacket and bib-fronted trousers of the Armored Force winter uniform as issued to tank crews, with the ubiquitous 'Cap, Wool, Knit M1941' better known as the 'beanie'. One wears the US 1st Army left shoulder patch.

1942, full 'hostilities only' commissions being granted on 26 February 1944. The corps reached a peak strength of 11,086, but by July 1947 demobilisation, poor retention and recruiting had left only 2,100 nurses in service. (The Navy was slower than the Army to accept black nurses, the first to enter the NNC only being taken on for active duty in April 1945.)

Entry requirements for the NNC ensured high professional standards. Candidates had to be graduates of a USN-approved nursing school, Registered Nurses, and US citizens for at least ten years. For the regular corps the age limits were 22 to 28, but reservists were accepted from the age of 21 to 40. Additionally, candidates were expected to be and to remain single, resigning from the corps upon marriage. This ruling was modified on 10 January 1945 due to the excessive losses of qualified nurses due to marriage; the new ruling allowed nurses to remain in service following marriage, but still barred married women from entering service. (Prior to this ruling an average of 100 nurses were resigning each month in order to marry, with a high point of 160 resignations in November 1944.) In February 1945 members who had resigned the service to marry between 1 January 1944 and 10 January 1945 were permitted to apply for temporary re-appointment with the corps. In September the new relaxed policy regarding marriage was rescinded, however; and in October a somewhat cynical announcement was made that with effect from 1 November all married nurses would be released from the service – thus conveniently disposing of excess nurses once the war was over without honouring the 'war's end plus six months' provision.

Uniforms From its inception the NNC had only a limited wardrobe, consisting of the hospital dress for duty wear, later supplemented by hat, sweater, cape and raincoat; these were the only prescribed uniform items until an outdoor uniform was first proposed in June 1941. The outdoor uniform was to be for use by personnel overseas or working under severe climatic conditions, and furthermore was to be obtained at the individual's own expense. The first of the new uniforms were procured in 1942. Similar to the uniform of the WAVES, it consisted of a navy blue double-breasted tunic with gold rank lace on the cuffs, gilt buttons, and the NNC oakleaf-and-anchor insignia on each lapel. It was worn with a matching skirt, black stockings and shoes, white shirt and black tie (see Plate F1). Grey gloves were optional, and were replaced in early 1945 by black gloves. The cap was not dissimilar to the male USN officer's cap but without a visor; it was worn with the NNC badge on the crown, and a gold lace chinstrap. The summer uniform consisted of a white, single-breasted, four-pocket tunic with three-button front, white skirt, shoes and cap cover. With the summer uniform rank was worn on shoulderboards instead of the cuffs.

The granting of full naval commissioned ranks in February 1944 led to the adoption of new uniform regulations the following August; the NNC device was removed from the collar points and, void of the lettering, was worn on the cuffs above the rank lace, like the other line and staff insignia of male officers. A new style of uniform

cap now had no chinstrap; on the 'set-up' front was a backing patch for the USN officer's cap badge authorised that May in place of the NNC insignia previously worn.

May 1944 also saw the authorisation of a smart slate grey dress or 'work uniform', worn with grey gloves, black shoes and beige stockings (from this date beige stockings also replaced the white ones previously worn with white service dress; from December 1944 they also replaced the black stockings worn with blue service dress). A grey overseas cap or the regulation service cap were worn with the grey uniform. In overseas stations where laundering facilities were limited nurses were authorised to use the WAVES blue/white striped seersucker dress, with distinctive insignia.

The US Navy had its own air evacuation service; the first training course started at Alameda, California, on 11 December 1944, the newly trained Flight Nurses and Navy Corpsmen passing out in January 1945. **NNC Flight Nurses** wore a green wool uniform in the same shade as naval aviators, consisting of slacks, a zip-front 'shirt', an 'Ike' jacket and a baseball cap. Navy Flight Nurse wings were gold-plated Navy style aviation wings with superimposed NNC insignia, measuring 2ins from wingtip to wingtip. Grey cotton uniforms of a similar style were also issued.

Navy Nurse Corps relative ranks (before February 1944)

NNC	USN
Superintendent	Captain
Assistant Superintendent	Commander
Director	Lieutenant-Commander
Assistant Director	Lieutenant
Chief Nurse	Lieutenant (Junior Grade)
Nurse	Ensign
Probationary Nurse	(officer status)

When wearing the white hospital dress the rank was displayed on the nursing cap, using the same sequence of gold stripes as worn on the outdoor uniform, corresponding to the equivalent USN ranks. Probationary Nurses wore no rank insignia.

Female medical officers

In April 1943, Congress announced that 'During the present war and for six months thereafter there shall be included in the Medical Departments of the Army and Navy such licensed female physicians and surgeons as the Secretary of War and the Secretary of the Navy may consider necessary'. These female officers were appointed as temporary Reserve officers of the Army or Navy with equal status. Women medical officers were employed by the US Army in the same manner as those in British service; they wore WAC uniform with Medical Corps caduceus insignia on the collar, and the US eagle cap badge on their visored service cap. By Army regulations they were expressly forbidden the use of the WAC off-duty dresses or the 'old gold' WAC scarf, which were considered distinctive items to that corps.

Litter cases stacked in three tiers in an air ambulance. The use of 'blues' by the nurse and the M1917A1 helmet by the medic suggest that this posed image was taken during one of the early air evacuation flights in 1943.

American Red Cross

During wartime nurses were enrolled in the American Red Cross Nursing Service as 'Reserves' of the Army or Navy Nurse Corps, enlisting in the ANC or NNC for an extendable period of at least one year. Under an Act of Congress originally passed in April 1908 the ARC had formed a nursing reserve for the Army and Navy since 1912; the ARC also had responsibility for the recruitment of ANC nurses and handled applicants for the NNC, although early in the war a small number were recruited following direct applications to the ANC and NNC. Later the NNC took over responsibility for its own recruiting, following suggestions that the ARC had perhaps overemphasised the needs of the Army at the expense of the Navy.

As an organisation in its own right the ARC filled a number of roles in support of both American civilians and the military, including assignment to the armed forces, blood donor service, nursing service, volunteer special services, nutrition service, disaster relief and the Junior Red Cross. The aid offered was as varied as it was widespread, and the plethora of insignia and dress distinctions associated with the different grades and services is a study in its own right. Services to the military were amongst the most important duties of the ARC – Red Cross welfare aides providing coffee and doughnuts to troops in transit may be the popular image of these ladies, but their contributions were tremendously varied and, like that of the British and Commonwealth VADs, essential to the war effort. By comparison with the VADs a greater emphasis was placed on providing for the general wellbeing of all troops rather than just the care of the wounded. In 1940, long before American entry into World War II, the American Hospital Great Britain opened a 300-bed hospital near Basingstoke, Hampshire; the following year the ARC opened a second 125-bed hospital near Salisbury, Wiltshire. **Uniform** See Plate E2.

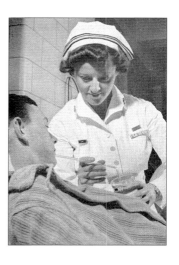

NNC Chief Nurse Ann Bernatitus gives fluid to a wounded 'gob' in a US Navy hospital; her rank of lieutenant junior grade is denoted by the one narrow above one broad stripes on the cap. Wearing the white ward dress, she sports the Distinguished Unit Citation bar on her right breast, and ribbons for the Legion of Merit, American Defense (with star) and Asiatic-Pacific Theater medals – these were awarded for service early in 1942 in Bataan and on Corregidor, from where she was ordered to escape aboard the submarine USS *Spearfish*. Many of her fellow nurses lost their lives in Japanese captivity.

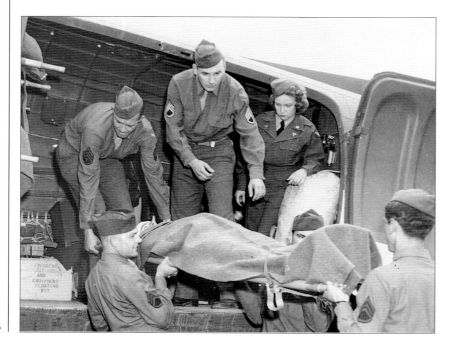

1944: a seriously wounded litter case is loaded into an aircraft of IX Troop Carrier Command; Medical Corps NCOs undertake the heavy lifting, watched by a Flight Nurse who is ready to provide whatever care may be needed during the flight. The nurse wears the later OD wool version of the formerly grey-blue wool F1 flying jacket, A1 slacks and C1 cap (cf Plate D2). Air evacuation aircraft rarely flew with red cross markings, since they were not exclusively for medical use. Many flew into isolated locations where the troops also needed every inch of cargo space available on incoming flights to bring in supplies of all kinds.

GREAT BRITAIN
1: Sister, QARNNS (Reserve); Royal Naval Hospital Stonehouse, UK, 1942
2: Lieutenant, Medical Branch, Royal Naval Volunteer Reserve;
   RNH Rosyth, 1943
3: Orderly, Voluntary Aid Detachment, British Red Cross;
   RAMC, Aldershot Garrison, 1943

A

1a

B

3a

1

2

3

GREAT BRITAIN
1: Lieutenant, RAMC: Aldershot, UK, 1944
2: Sister, PMRAFNS; Ely, UK, 1943
3: Cpl. Nursing Orderly, WAAF; air evacuation
   unit, Normandy, June 1944

C

UNITED STATES
1: Captain, ANC; 91st General Hospital, England, 1943
2: Lieutenant, ANC; 806th MAE Sqn, England, 1943
3: Nurse, ANC; 179th Station Hospital, Adak Island, Aleutians, 1943

D

UNITED STATES
1: Lieutenant, ANC; 313th Station Hospital,
   England, 1944
2: 'Gray Lady', American Red Cross;
   USA, 1944
3: Hospital Aide, Women's Army Corps;
   USA, 1945

E

UNITED STATES & CANADA
1: Lieutenant (JG), US NNC; 12th Base Hospital, England, March 1944
2: Sister, Royal Canadian Navy Hospital Avalon, Newfoundland, 1943
3: Sister, Royal Canadian Army Medical Corps; Liri Valley, Italy, spring 1944

AUSTRALIA, NEW ZEALAND & INDIA
1: Sister, Australian ANS; general hospital, New Guinea, 1943
2: Sister, New Zealand NS; casualty clearing station, Libya, 1942
3: Sister, Indian MNS; field hospital, Burma, 1944

USSR, FRANCE & BELGIUM
1: Red Army Doctor 3rd Class; Russia, 1941
2: Adjudant, nursing section, Corps des Voluntaires Françaises; London, 1942
3: Sister, Belgian Army; England, 1940

Volunteers of the American Red Cross parade before their HQ building. All wear a smart double-breasted dress with breast and hip pockets, and the overseas cap. The variety of civilian belts suggest that none was issued with this uniform, but that its use improved the appearance of the female figure.

TOP A recruiting poster for the US Navy Nurse Corps – a smart uniform and a pretty girl were enticing images, enabling the NNC to reach a peak wartime strength of 11,086 nurses.

ABOVE A contrasting ANC poster varies the approach for attracting volunteers, playing on emotions aroused by the dark sky and war-torn city in the background and the dutiful poise of the nurse. She wears the white ward dress and blue corridor cape with its traditional red lining.

BRITISH COMMONWEALTH

Canadian Nursing Services

The first nurses to serve with the Canadian military were those sent to provide care for the casualties of the North-West Rebellion of May 1885; this was to result in proposals for the formation of a Canadian Army Nursing Service. In 1899 four Canadian nurses embarked for South Africa with the first Canadian Contingent, being paid and provided for as lieutenants. In 1901 the service became an integral part of the Canadian Army Medical Corps, though with a very small full-time cadre (only five prior to World War I); this was to be rapidly supplemented by reservists in time of war.

During World War II, nurses of the Royal Canadian Army Medical Corps served in Tunisia, Sicily, Italy, Great Britain and NW Europe as well as in hospitals in Canada. The RCAMC nursing service was senior to those of the RCN and RCAF, the latter two being formed during the war and never attaining the scale achieved by the Army. A total of 343 nurses were to serve with the Royal Canadian Navy during 1942–45; these women were mainly to see service at home, although a few did serve at RCNH *Niobe* at Greenock in Scotland. From the start RCN nurses held equivalent RCN ranks. The RCAF nurses served mainly in Canada, although two served with an RCAF field hospital in Normandy. A number of RCAF nurses received air evacuation training with the Americans at Bowman Field in Kentucky, but in the event their training and skills were wasted – an interpretation of RCAF orders meant that no women were to fill any posts involving flying duties, despite the fact that the RAF had allowed them to do so.

Battledress as well as Khaki Drill blouse, skirt and slacks were issued for field use as needed (see Plate F3). The basic ward dress of all three services was similar, being differentiated only by insignia of rank and service. Outdoor dress was similar to that worn by the corresponding British services. In RCAF service the outdoor uniform or service dress was the 4A Dress authorised for wear in messes, when socialising, on temporary duty or in an administrative post. The 4A Dress was similar to the blue-grey wool tunic and skirt worn by the PMRAFNS. The 4B was a stylised ward dress consisting of a tunic, skirt, veil and belt; in its basic form it was worn by all three services (see Plate F2). It was permitted to be worn on all occasions, and with a white apron for ward duty (except by Matrons and Senior Sisters). The 4C Dress consisted of a typical nurse's white cotton dress with buttoning waistbelt and veil; in bad weather it was worn with a corridor cape.

Section 6, Chapter 6 of RCAF Dress Regulations, April 1944, is perhaps worth quoting as a representative example of the obsessively detailed thought given by military nursing services of the 1940s to the question of female appearance:

'140. Hair
(a) The hair is to be kept free of the collar at all times when in uniform.
(b) There is not to be more than 1½ inches of hair showing while on duty.
(c) No hair is to show at the back of the veil.
(d) The veil is to be secured to the head invisibly.

141. Makeup and nail polish to be inconspicuous.'

In 1942 the previously relative ranks became equal in all respects to those of the Regular forces – the first Allied nursing service to be so recognised. RCN and RCAF rank corresponded to that of the RCAMC and the equivalent RCN/RCAF ranks.

RCAMC Nursing Service relative ranks

Matron-in-Chief	Lieutenant-colonel
Principal Matron	Major
Matron	Captain
Nursing Sister (after 6 months)	Lieutenant
Nursing Sister (under training)	2nd Lieutenant

Australian Army Nursing Service

The AANS was formed in 1898, and 26 nursing sisters saw service in South Africa during the Boer War. The contribution made by the nurses was recognised in 1902 when the service received official status, and confirmed in 1903 when they became a Reserve of the Australian Army Medical Corps. Appointment qualifications were similar to those of British military nurses; the candidate had to be a British subject, not less than 21 years of age or more than 40, unmarried, and a nurse registered in one of the states or territories of the Australian Commonwealth. Once appointed, relative rank and badges were granted, but commissions were not awarded and military titles were not used.

The AANS was mobilised on 4 September 1939, with the first detachment proceeding overseas – to Palestine – in January 1940. In all 4,220 Australian nurses served the armed forces during World War II; of these 3,484 were members of the AANS. Australian nurses served in the Middle East, Greece, Crete, Syria, Malaya and New Guinea as well as continental Australia, incurring a number of casualties on active service. The title 'Royal' was granted in 1948.

Nurses of the Royal Canadian Army Medical Corps photographed in England, c.1943. All wear the tri-service tunic and skirt in mid-blue gabardine with white collar and cuffs (cf Plate F2). The lancer-fronted tunic had a single pocket off-set to the right in which a white handkerchief was always displayed. These nurses are recognisable as Army sisters by the ranking on their epaulettes, and the brown leather belt with a gilt clasp bearing a silver crown (see Plate F3). A 'Norfolk'-cut service uniform in navy blue was worn for walking out.

New Guinea was a particularly unpleasant environment, especially when wearing the ward dress; despite moves to replace it with more suitable clothing it was still very much to be seen as late as 1944. On the right here is WAAAF Section Officer Allen, in blue service cap, KD shirt and slacks, web anklets and brown boots. At left, Matron Wheatley wears the RAAFNS white tropical ward dress with full-length nine-button front, and 'trilby' hat. An issue of the KD as worn by the WAAAF would have been far more comfortable, but was considered not to be in keeping with the high standards of appearance then expected of a nurse.

The US Army's 12th Station Hospital, Townsville, Australia, 1942: American doctors and ANC nurses wheel a GI from the operating room to the recovery ward. Both nurses wear the 'Uniform, Nurse's, Cotton, Blue' initially worn as ward dress outside the continental USA. Once replaced by the brown/white seersucker dress, this uniform was later used by WAC Hospital Aides.

As with the other Commonwealth nursing services, the uniform of the AANS was based on that of the British services, with a grey trilby hat and grey ward dress bearing red epaulettes. Rank insignia were worn on the epaulettes in bronze, with a curved 'AUSTRALIA' title at the base. A silver Australian Commonwealth Military Forces 'rising sun and crown' badge, based upon that worn by Army ranks but smaller, was worn at the throat of the tippet. Nurses serving in the South-West Pacific initially wore the grey ward dress; unsuited to tropical service, this was supplemented in 1943 by an issue of a broad-brimmed bush hat, KD tunic and slacks or a one-piece KD coverall (see Plate G1). Male pattern jungle green uniform also saw limited use.

The medical services of the Royal Australian Air Force and Royal Australian Navy were organised on the same lines as those of the AANS although on a much smaller scale, with only 660 RAAF nurses and 60 RAN nurses serving during World War II. As with Great Britain and other Commonwealth nations, Australian female doctors served with the RAAF on equal pay and status to male officers. Similarly, 21 women doctors saw service with the Australian Army Medical Corps, which also employed specialist women physiotherapists who were appointed as lieutenants in the AAMC.

Formed in December 1942, the **Australian Army Medical Women's Service** had a similar role to that of the British Mobile VAD – a role originally fulfilled by Australian VAD units. The increased requirement for personnel within the medical services, particularly in administrative duties, led to the formation of the AAMWS as an auxiliary service of the Australian Army Medical Corps. The initial roll of 5,000 women were provided mainly by VAD members transferring directly to the new service. Unlike the VAD, the AAMWS served under similar terms and conditions to those of the other military women's auxiliary services (to which they were junior), with comparative pay scales; members of the AAMWS were addressed as 'nursing orderly'. Part-time voluntary VAD members continued to serve in a limited capacity in their home areas only.

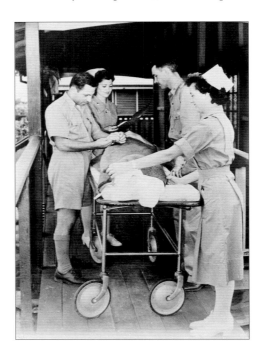

New Zealand Army Nursing Service

The mass call-up of trained nurses during the Great War had caused severe disruption to the civil nursing services; they lost many of their senior nursing staff, which further disrupted training of new nurses. Before the outbreak of war in 1939 the New Zealand government were keen to ensure that the problems of 1914–18 were not repeated, and in June 1939 a Nursing Council was set up to administer the increase in nursing staff which would be required by any future war. One important ruling of the council was that key civilian nurses could be accepted onto a waiting list for the military nursing services, but were unable to join up unless a satisfactory replacement was found. A number of NZANS sisters served overseas during World War II, some being stationed in England and later in Greece, the Middle East and the Pacific; 11 of them were to give their lives in service of their country.

At the outbreak of World War II the status of NZ nurses was much the same as those in other Commonwealth nations; however, with effect from 30 June 1941 members of the NZANS were entitled to wear Army-style rank (but smaller insignia than those worn by male officers). From 1942 they were to receive commissioned status with equivalent rank for the duration of the war. NZ Army Order 62/1943 gave further notification that nursing staff would from that time come under military law. The NZANS also provided nursing staff to the Royal New Zealand Air Force, which had no nursing organisation of its own; a total of 55 Army nurses were to serve with the RNZAF, and signified their attachment by the use of the bracketed word '(Air)' after their rank. The RNZAF nurses were supported by 119 VAD staff. The first three nurses to serve with the Royal New Zealand Navy were seconded from the civilian health service; in March 1943 two of these staff were appointed to the NZANS and the third was replaced by a NZANS sister, the three then being attached for duty with the navy. Only five NZANS personnel were to serve on secondment to the RNZN during the war.

The basic NZANS outdoor uniform was similar to the grey 'Norfolk' tunic and skirt worn by members of the QAIMNS prior to 1944; however, unlike the British, the New Zealanders retained this uniform throughout the war. A grey double-breasted overcoat was available for winter wear; both summer and winter dress was worn with a grey felt trilby-style hat with a silk band, later replaced by a beret. The ward dress ('nurse's over-alls') consisted of a white knee-length dress, and later a grey field dress (see Plate G2), both types being worn

Tropical whites, with a felt trilby hat and red epaulettes of rank, worn by a sister of the New Zealand Army Nursing Service in the SW Pacific. A similar uniform was issued to most Commonwealth nursing services, but its use was usually limited to base areas, as it was easily soiled and needed frequent laundering.

A fine studio portrait of an Australian volunteer serving with the American Red Cross; the ARC recruited locally when stationed with US troops in Allied countries. Foreign volunteers wore their national title at the shoulder of the blue-grey 'outdoor' uniform; British volunteers also added a crown to the metal 'ARC' title worn on both collars.

OPPOSITE **The extreme conditions endured in Burma are aptly illustrated by this image of an American forward jungle hospital, looking more like a native village. (Although there was only one US ground unit in Burma – 'Merrill's Marauders' – the USAAF provided combat and transport units to support British, Commonwealth and Chinese forces, so American hospitals were also present.) Despite the very basic setting of the hospital such forward medical facilities were essential to the survival of many seriously wounded casualties who could not easily be moved. US hospitals in Burma were largely staffed by Chinese nurses.**

with a white veil. For tropical use a white tricolene dress was issued and worn with a white felt trilby.

RNZANS relative ranks post-1942

Matron-in-Chief	Colonel
Principal Matron	Lieutenant-Colonel
Matron	Major
Assistant or Charge Sister	Captain
Sister	Lieutenant

The rank of Staff Nurse had been abolished in November 1941. Prior to the use of Army-style badges, rank had been shown by red braid on the cuff of the ward dress, e.g. one, two and three stripes of half-inch braid for Staff Nurse, Sister and Sister-in-Charge respectively.

South African Military Nursing Service

The SAMNS came into existence at the start of World War I; its members gave distinguished service throughout the Great War but, in common with many service assets, it was all but disbanded during the inter-war years – by 1939 there were only 14 serving nursing sisters, only one of whom was a Regular. Emergency cover was provided by a Reserve system whereby 10 per cent of civilian nurses were released from their hospitals or organisations in time of war or national emergency to serve with the SAMNS, these forming the nucleus of a service that would be expanded by additional volunteers. South African nurses served outside the Union including North Africa, Italy, the Middle East and on the hospital ship *Amra*. The SAMNS was very stretched by its wartime commitments, the problem being partially rectified during 1943 when over 300 Canadian nurses were provided for service in South Africa.

SAMNS relative ranks

Matron-in-Chief	Colonel
Principal Matron	Lieutenant-Colonel
Senior & Junior Matron	Major
Trained Nurses, Physiotherapists & Radiographers	Captain
Probationer Nursing Assistants, Dental Nursing Assts, Radiographer Nursing Assts	2nd Lieutenant
Cadets & other probationers	(officer status)

SOVIET UNION

The Soviets were not signatories of the Geneva Conventions in their entirety, allowing them a degree of flexibility and interpretation in the use of their medical staff. Revolutionary Military Council Order No.798 of 25 July 1925 had stated that 'The personnel of military-sanitary units, establishments and institutions of the Workers' and Peasants' Red Army (RKKA) and Fleet in wartime' were to have an armband 'with the image of the Red Cross on a white background, and the mark of the establishment to which a serviceman is assigned or attached.' To have worn the armband would have meant that medics could not have fought as riflemen; thus the red cross armband was not then normally encountered in Soviet service.

On 25 August 1931 the USSR signed the part of the Geneva Conventions dated 27 July 1929, covering the fate of wounded and sick; and consequently Order No.169 was issued on 5 September 1932, covering the application of the Conventions in the Red Army. This stated: 'Personnel of the military-sanitary service of the RKKA should have an armband with the image of the Red Cross on a white background with the mark of the Military-Sanitary Directorate of the RKKA, on the left sleeve above the elbow'.

Under the savage conditions of the Eastern Front, 1941–45, the evacuation of the wounded, and their subsequent treatment, was a hit-and-miss process often limited by local tactical conditions and shortages. The Red Army's chain of evacuation was largely based upon the Western system, and except for periods of rapid retreat or advance their base hospitals tended to be closer to the front lines than was normal in the West. If there was a difference in practice, it was that classification of casualties for dispersal to various

specialised field surgical units depending on the nature of their wounds tended to happen earlier in the chain of evacuation. Despite the apparent risks of this system in cases of multiple wounds – highly characteristic of 20th-century warfare – the Russians claimed that giving only superficial treatment at the front and passing men rapidly back down the chain substantially reduced mortality.

Hospitals were often relatively primitive and poorly equipped, however. There were few comforts for patients, who received only the most basic rations; the attitude of the authorities was governed by the cold calculation that the wounded – being no longer useful as fighting men – should enjoy a lower priority than the able-bodied. This was, of course, off-set in countless individual cases by the devotion of dedicated doctors and nurses.

In Red Army service nurses held enlisted rank, the highest being that of *starshina* (sergeant-major) – although all ranks were collectively referred to as *myedsyestra* (medical sister). Air force nursing rank and structure was the same as in the rest of the RKKA, of which the Red Air Force – VVS – was an integral branch. Unlike the other Allied nations, the Soviets employed women as front line medical orderlies, serving with rifle companies, and actually armed with infantry weapons. These women were often very young, former medical students or even high school graduates with the most basic first aid training and equipment. Moreover, their task began with physically dragging and carrying the wounded out of danger. One example was the 20-year-old Gulya Koroleva, who served with the 214th Rifle Division in the 24th Army on the northern flank of the Stalingrad front in winter 1942/43; Koroleva was posthumously awarded the Order of the Red Banner for bringing more than 100 wounded men out of the line, and killing 15 of the enemy herself.

OPPOSITE **Two Red Army medical officers pose in typically mixed uniform styles of the second half of the war, reflecting the January 1943 regulations (cf.Plate H1). The lieutenant at left wears the dark blue M1941 beret with metal red star badge. Her pale khaki, right-buttoning male pattern M1943 *gymnastiorka* has a stand collar, and detachable shoulderboards of khaki 'field' quality, outlined with red piping, with a single green medical branch rank stripe flanked by two subdued rank stars at the outer end; damage makes it difficult to tell, but under magnification she seems to display the serpent-and-chalice medical branch emblem centrally. Note the Guards unit badge over the right breast; the old-style two-prong frame belt buckle (women officers might be excused the cross strap in a concession to the female figure); and what seems to be the khaki field uniform skirt.**

At right is a one-star junior lieutenant wearing a *pilotka* in a dark shade; since the edge-piping of her narrow shoulderboards appears to be black, the cap may be in the steel grey of M1935 armoured troops' uniform. The parade quality shoulderboards looped to the shoulders of her khaki, left-buttoning female pattern *gymnastiorka* are in silver lace with black edging, the green medical rank stripe, and a single gold rank star, but no branch emblem. (Courtesy Lászlo Békési)

These women faced exactly the same perils as any other Red Army soldier, and very large numbers lost their lives on the battlefield and in captivity; Germany did not extend the protection of the Geneva Conventions to Soviet prisoners of war. Twelve women medical personnel were to receive the Soviet Union's highest decoration for gallantry, the gold star of Hero of the Soviet Union.

Female doctors served alongside male colleagues as medical officers, and were ranked in non-combat branches in 'classes', with e.g. a 'doctor 3rd class' being equivalent to a captain; in the combat arms medical personnel used normal military rank titles. (In wartime command appointments were often held by quite junior ranks – e.g. a captain might command a medical battalion.) **Uniforms** See commentary, Plate H1.

Red Fleet nurses wore the same uniform as that worn by male ratings, their employment being identified by a circular badge on the upper left sleeve; this *sanitar* insignia consisted of an embroidered red cross within a circle on a black or white backing (to match the winter or summer uniform). Ratings with the ranks of petty officer 1st and 2nd class, CPO and *mishman* (midshipman) had arm badges with a yellow circular border and red cross. Officers of the naval medical branch had silver rank lace and cap badges and, after the January 1943 uniform regulations, silver cap cords and lace to the cap's visor where appropriate.

SELECT BIBLIOGRAPHY

Beevor, Antony, *Stalingrad,* Penguin Books (1999)

Brayley, Martin J., ill.Bujeiro, Ramiro, *World War II Allied Women's Services,* Men-at-Arms 357, Osprey Publishing (2001)

Brayley, Martin J. & Ingram, Richard, *World War II British Women's Uniforms,* Crowood Press (1995 & 2001)

Burke-Fessler, Diane, *No Time For Fear,* Michigan State University Press (1996)

Collet Wadge, D., *Women in Uniform,* Sampson Lowe (1946)

Cormack, Andrew, *The Royal Air Force 1939–45,* Men-at-Arms 225, Osprey Publishing (1990)

Cotterell, Anthony, *R.A.M.C.,* Hutchinson & Co.(c.1943)

Ellis, John, *World War II: The Sharp End,* Windrow & Greene (1990)

Feller, Lt.Col.& Moore, Major, *Highlights in the History of the Army Nurse Corps,* US Army (1995)

Laffin, John, *Combat Surgeons,* J.M.Dent & Sons (1970)

Rottman, Gordon, ill.Chin, Francis, *US Army Air Force (2),* Elite 51, Osprey Publishing (1994)

Sterner, Doris M., *In and Out of Harm's Way,* Peanut Butter (1997)

Official Guide to the Army Air Forces, Bonanza Books (1944)

HMSO, WO, & various other period publications

MILITARIA Magazine, Paris – various articles, esp. Paul Gaujac, 'Femmes Françaises sous l'Uniforme 1940–43', *Militaria* No.161

THE PLATES

A: GREAT BRITAIN

A1: Sister, Queen Alexandra's Royal Naval Nursing Service (Reserve); Royal Naval Hospital Stonehouse, UK, 1942

The ward dress of QARNNS sisters was amongst the smartest of the military nursing services: a dark blue dress with white apron and veil, red cuffs, and blue tippet with red trim. This sister is in formal dress, as shown by the white cotton gloves. The blue fabric belt was normally worn with this dress, although the white belt generally worn with tropical uniform is seen in some photographs. On the lower right front of the tippet this sister wears a rank badge embroidered on a black patch. This showed a king's crown, above an anchor entwined with Queen Alexandra's 'AA' monogram in red, above a circular red cross badge. The rank of SNS was indicated by a red bar beneath the red cross; of SS, by a red border round the patch; of Matron, by a gold border; of Principal Matron, by a gold border and two gold bars; and of Matron-in-Chief, by a double gold border. QARNNS Reserve badges were embroidered in silver wire, with the word 'RESERVE' at the bottom of the patch; Regular QARNNS nurses had the rank badge embroidered in gold. At the lower rear corner of the veil the naval crown was embroidered in blue; similarly, PMRAFNS wore RAF wings and Army nurses wore the insignia of their parent organisation in the same location.

A2: Lieutenant, Medical Branch, Royal Naval Volunteer Reserve; RNH Rosyth, 1943

The first female medical officer had been a member of the WRNS, but she was later transferred to the RNVR, after which all female MOs joined as members of the RNVR and held naval rather than WRNS rank. This doctor wears basically WRNS officer's uniform: a navy blue (virtually black) double-breasted jacket and box-pleated skirt, a black felt tricorn hat, white shirt, black tie, stockings and shoes. The MO's uniform differed from that of the WRNS in having RNVR ('wavy navy') rank lace separated by the scarlet of the medical branch, and the gold embroidered RN officer's cap badge. Very few female medical officers were appointed. The 'outdoor' uniform worn by members of the QARNNS and QARNNS(R) from 1942 was similar, but differed in having the distinctive QARNNS rank patch worn on epaulettes and, without its rank elements, as the cap badge.

A3: Orderly, Voluntary Aid Detachment, British Red Cross; RAMC, Aldershot, 1943

VAD orderlies wore the uniform of their parent organisation, in this case the Red Cross. All the 'outdoor' uniforms were similar, of navy blue barathea or comparable fabric with a simple A-line skirt; a gabardine cap; white or blue shirt, and black tie, stockings and shoes. The parent organisation was identified by distinctive badges. This VAD orderly wears the Red Cross cap badge on the cap, which is of the same shape as the PMRAFNS 'storm cap'. Arc-shaped brass shoulder titles of the organisation and county names surround a detachment numeral (e.g. 'RED CROSS/49/LONDON'). This VAD is further identified as being attached for duty with the Royal Army Medical Corps by the RAMC cap badge worn on the left breast in the same manner as ATS personnel, in bronze for officers and brass for other ranks. At least four different types of headwear were to be seen in use during the war: a straw summer hat, a felt trilby worn by officers, the 'storm cap' shown here, and a soft peaked cap based on that worn by the ATS. Organisation and rank were further identified by the cap band ribbon, which was blue with a white upper edge for BRC members but had an added red trim for officers. **(Inset, A3a)** The 'Mobile' badge worn on the left forearm shows that this orderly has volunteered for employment anywhere in the world where she may be called upon to serve.

B: GREAT BRITAIN

B1: Sister, Queen Alexandra's Imperial Military Nursing Service (Reserve); London, 1943

Scarlet and grey were the traditional colours of the Army nursing services, and this was reflected in both ward and 'outdoor' uniforms, which were grey with scarlet trim. This sister of the QAIMNS(R) wears the outdoor uniform of traditional 'Norfolk' cut, with a buttoned belt. The collar has broad scarlet edging and silver QAIMNS(R) badges **(inset B1a)**, and bronze lieutenant's rank 'pips' are displayed on the epaulettes. The shirt is white, the tie and stockings light grey and the shoes black, of the same pattern as the other women's services. Headgear was originally a grey felt trilby, but it was decided that this was not well suited to wartime use, and in 1943 this new cap was adopted; identical in design to that worn by the ATS, it too bears the badge shown at B1a. Procurement of the grey fabric became a problem, and it was decided that with effect from January 1944 the Army nursing services would change into khaki. The new uniform, modelled on that worn by ATS officers, more readily identified nurses as Army officers; the cap and collar badges were retained, and in reference to their prized traditional colours a double scarlet and grey lanyard was adopted at the right shoulder.

B2: Sister, Territorial Army Nursing Service; Normandy, June 1944

Army nurses soon discovered that the grey ward dress was not well suited to active service, which – in the advanced surgical centres and field hospitals in North Africa – might

British Army nurses in Normandy queue for a meal. They wear a mixture of male and ATS pattern BD uniform, GS caps and steel helmets, and khaki or white Geneva Cross brassards on the left sleeve (cf Plate B2).

require them to dive into a slit trench during an air raid, or clamber into lorries for a rapid advance or withdrawal. Authorisation for suitable clothing was slow in coming, but eventually nurses managed to acquire KD slacks and jacket or shirt; serge Battledress also made an appearance, but was male issue, which left much to be desired in the matter of fitting. By summer 1944 all the nurses being sent to the advanced hospitals in Normandy were wearing BD – some was ATS issue, but due to shortages many nurses once again had to use badly fitting male pattern BD. This recently arrived TANS sister queues for her first meal since arrival in Normandy, still wearing the Pattern 37 web equipment issued for carriage of her kit: belt, braces, brace attachments, large pack worn on the back, small pack at the left side, and waterbottle. Nurses received the same basic field kit as male personnel, meals being eaten out of messtins. The steel helmet was worn or kept close at hand – the beachhead was subject to shelling and air raids. When out of the line the 'Cap, General Service' was standard field wear for nurses – and as unpopular with them as with everyone else. On her sleeve this sister wears the red cross armband, providing protection to all medical staff under the terms of the Geneva Conventions. Above this is the blue cross on red shield of 21st Army Group – later, of British troops in France. The ribbon of the Africa Star indicates that this nurse is no stranger to the discomforts of field service.

B3: Sister, Queen Alexander's Imperial Military Nursing Service (Reserve); base hospital, France, 1945

The ward dress echoed the 'prim and proper' perception of the military nurse, but the only alternative to this for active service had been BD, leaving a practical vacuum between the two extremes of uniform. To bridge the gap the 'Dress, Field Force, Nursing Officer's' was introduced for use by nurses in operational theatres. Less smart than the formal grey ward dress, but infinitely more befitting than Battledress in forward hospitals, the field dress was a welcome addition to the nurse's wardrobe. It had button-on removable long sleeves for use in both cool and warm climates; it was easily cleaned in the laundering facilities available at every hospital unit; and it had integral epaulettes on which rank could be displayed when the tippet was laid aside – note the bronze 'pips' and scarlet edging. Despite the relaxed style of the field force dress it was normally worn with a well-starched and pressed white veil.

C: GREAT BRITAIN

C1: Lieutenant, Royal Army Medical Corps; Aldershot, UK, 1944

The Army was quick to realise the benefits of employing female doctors, who could treat patients of both sexes and were essential in the care of female ranks, particularly at larger ATS depots or recruiting centres. The fact that only 150 women medical officers were employed by the RAMC during the war simply reflected the far smaller numbers of female doctors graduated by the civilian medical schools in the 1930s–40s in comparison with today. Uniform was that worn by ATS officers, but as they were full members of the RAMC, corps buttons, cap and collar badges were used, and in this instance the coloured Field Service cap with gilt badge. Unlike the ATS, female medical officers wore the

A WAAF corporal nursing orderly attends to wounded Canadian soldiers before their air evacuation from Normandy, June 1944. She wears the WAAF service cap, Battledress-style 'working suit', and a round-necked sweater (cf Plate C3). In the background a C-47 Dakota bearing invasion stripes, but no Geneva Cross emblems, awaits its load of wounded.

Sam Browne complete with the shoulder strap. This doctor, ranking as a lieutenant, holds the King's Commission and has equal status and pay to her male colleagues.

C2: Sister, Princess Mary's Royal Air Force Nursing Service; Ely, UK, 1943

This nursing officer, with the RAF rank of flying officer (equivalent to lieutenant), wears the so-called 'summer' service dress of the PMRAFNS, in fine RAF blue-grey barathea. The tunic is of the same 'Norfolk' cut as Plate B1, with a box-pleated three-button front, a buttoned integral belt and deep hip pockets set to the sides. From March 1943 conventional RAF officers' rank lace was worn on the cuffs in place of the coloured 'appointment lace' previously worn. The collar points display the RAF medical service winged caduceus device (inset C3a). The six-gore skirt, noticeably longer than wartime fashion, was also authorised for wear with the BD-style blouse of the 'Suit, Working, WAAF' for field use – although the far more practical WAAF slacks were substituted whenever possible. The black felt hat is similar to the tricorn worn by WRNS senior rates and officers, but is in fact four-cornered. For less formal wear a 'storm cap' was used.

C3: Corporal Nursing Orderly, WAAF; air evacuation unit, Normandy, June 1944

Air evacuation staff were drawn from both PMRAFNS sisters and WAAF nursing orderlies. This orderly waiting by her C-47 Dakota on a windswept airstrip in the Normandy beachhead wears the normal flying clothing: the WAAF's BD-style 'Suit, Working' worn over a round-necked blue-grey sweater, and her service cap. She has been issued the 'observer's' parachute harness (i.e. for use with a separately stowed clip-on parachute pack) and a 'Mae West' lifevest. WAAF leather ankle boots are worn here; sheepskin flying boots could frequently be seen worn on top of these due to the large size of the latter. As a member of the RAF medical branch she has the caduceus badge on both collar points of her blouse, and a red cross brassard on the left arm. Although specially trained as an orderly she is not a fully qualified nurse; the RAF considered this unnecessary, given the short duration of most air evacuation flights in NW Europe and the usual presence of a nursing sister in the same crew.

(Inset C3a) The RAF medical service device; this was in brass for enlisted ranks and gilt for officers – fine quality private purchase examples were available with overlaid silver wings on a gilt base. The device was worn by all medical officers, doctors, nursing orderlies and nurses.

D: UNITED STATES

D1: Captain, Army Nurse Corps; Churchill (91st General) Hospital, Oxford, England, 1943

This ANC nursing officer assigned to the 8th USAAF – note her Army Air Forces left shoulder patch – wears the service and walking-out uniform consisting of the 'Coat, Wool, Covert, Blue, Nurse's' with the 'Skirt, Wool, Covert, Blue, Nurse's' in contrasting shades. The unpopular cap originally furnished with the uniform was soon replaced with this overseas-style 'Cap, Garrison, Nurse's, Blue'. Note the maroon Medical Corps piping on the cap and epaulettes, and the maroon officers' cuff braid. She wears the caduceus department badge (see Plate E1a) on the left of the cap and her two silver rank bars on the right; the former is repeated on the lapels, below the cut-out 'U.S.' badges, and the latter on the epaulettes. The ribbon of the American Defense Medal but not yet that of the ETO Medal shows that she is not long in Britain.

In bad weather this uniform was supplemented by a smart double-breasted woollen 'Overcoat, Wool, Covert, Blue, Removable Lining, Nurse's' – which was in fact in even shorter supply than the uniform. A new OD uniform was proposed in late 1942 and authorised for overseas use in 1943 but, as with the blues, its initial procurement was slow.

D2: Lieutenant, Army Nurse Corps; 806th Medical Air Evacuation Squadron, Welford Park, England, 1943

Air evacuation flights were an essential aid to the survival of serious casualties in need of specialised care. Flight nurses flew in both C-47 Dakotas and C-54 Skymasters; such flights saved countless lives during the invasion of NW Europe – the lifts from Normandy began as early as 10 June, and during the first two months nearly 26,000 wounded

were evacuated by IX Troop Carrier Command. Transatlantic flights were undertaken from Prestwick, Scotland (which freak local weather conditions usually keep clear even when the rest of the UK is 'socked in'), with 24 litter patients flown back to the US in each C-54.

This nurse of the 806th MAES wears the F1 so-called 'flying jacket' and matching A1 slacks in a dark blueish-grey shade (an A1 skirt was also available) and the C1 cap – items specifically for issue to flight nurses. Note the maroon cap piping, with the fold on the right rather than the left as worn by D1; the lieutenant's silver rank bar on cap and epaulettes; and the single brass officers' 'U.S.' and Medical Corps caduceus on her right and left collar points respectively. On her left breast she wears the gold Flight Nurse wings; a small-scale version of male aircrew wings, they were replaced by an identical type but in sterling silver from September 1944.

The blue-grey flying garments were replaced by identical items made from standard US Army OD wool fabric in 1944. Suited to low-altitude flights in warmer climates, the basic uniform was supplemented by often grossly oversized male flight clothing, including e.g. the shearling B3 jacket, A5 trousers and A6 winter flying shoes. The shearling garments were later replaced by the standardised women's intermediate flying suit of B17 jacket and A13 slacks; made of a close-weave OD cotton cloth and lined with alpaca pile, they were produced in size ranges specific to women's needs. A lightweight flying suit – the OD gabardine L1 cap, L1 slacks

In the grounds of a former lunatic asylum pressed into service as an EMS hospital at Arlesey, Bedfordshire, in summer 1940, a VAD poses in ward dress. Subsequently a 'new style' dress was issued, with a rounded collar and elbow-length sleeves. The red cross was worn on the veil and apron. This nurse was sent first to do unskilled work in a London hospital; as she picked up experience and on-the-job training she progressed, and served as an operating theatre nurse at RNH Plymouth during the 1940/41 Blitz. The first words addressed to her by the naval surgeon who later became her husband were 'Here, nurse, get rid of this' – as he handed her a seaboot containing the mangled leg he had just amputated. (Courtesy Alice Shepherd)

and L1 jacket – was introduced for wear in climates ranging from 50 to 86 degrees F, and an identical uniform in khaki cotton – the K1 – was issued for temperatures above 97 degrees. Both the L1 and K1 sets were standardised in January 1945.

(Inset D2a) The first pattern USAAF Flight Nurse wings, authorised on 13 August 1943, were manufactured in solid hallmarked gold and measured 2ins from wingtip to wingtip.

D3: Nurse, Army Nurse Corps; 179th Station Hospital, Adak Island, Aleutians, 1943

Once the initial inertia and confusion had been overcome the task of clothing the women of the US armed forces received due attention. Production of WAC and ANC uniform was co-ordinated, the same items being issued to both services where possible. One example of this co-ordination was the cold weather parka; the issued item was identical for both services but was labelled as either the 'Overcoat, Nurse, Cold Climate, Parka Type' or the 'Overcoat, Women's, Parka Type'. (A drawback of this decision was that the different stock numbering and naming of the identical garments undoubtedly led to overstocking by quartermasters supplying both ANC and WAC personnel.) The parka had a warm alpaca fleece lining with a windproof cotton shell, a detachable hood and waistbelt. Under field conditions complaints were received about the fastening – a five-button front with a storm flap secured by three press studs; the studs tore away from the fabric too easily, the short shanks of the buttons made them insecure, and the bottom button was at waist level leaving the lower front open. These faults were not rectified, but the garment did at least offer better protection than had previously been available. Coming back cheerfully from 'mail call', this nurse exiled to the Aleutians in winter wears her parka with a knit 'beanie' cap, probably a male issue 'M41' field jacket, ill-fitting men's HBTs, OD wool gloves with brown leather palms and metal-snapped black cloth and rubber 'Overshoes, Arctic, Women's, 4-Buckle'.

E: UNITED STATES

E1 Lieutenant, Army Nurse Corps; 313th Station Hospital, Fremington, England, 1944

By June 1944 the US Army had 133,000 medical personnel and 84,210 beds distributed amongst 75 general and station hospitals throughout Britain. This lieutenant wears the OD winter uniform authorised for all nurses stationed outside the continental USA in 1943, and all nurses worldwide as from June 1944. Manufactured in a dark 'chocolate' shade with a matching skirt, service cap and garrison cap, and worn with flesh-coloured stockings and russet shoes, it was a part of the co-ordination plan to bring nurses' uniform into line with that of the WAC (and like WAC officers, nurses could alternatively wear the skirt in regulation 'pink'). Standardisation did not extend to handbags, the oblong 'Bag, Utility, Nurse's' carried here being distinctive to the ANC; also known as a purse, this was introduced as a standard item on 14 December 1942, following rejection of the WAAC pattern utility bag. As with all women's items, it was some time before supply met demand, and civilian bags remained in use in the meantime. The lieutenant wears the standard US Army officer's gilt badge on the service cap, OD officer's braid on the tunic cuffs, and collar and epaulette insignia as illustrated on the blue uniform, Plate D1.

US ANC nurses board a ship headed for mainland Europe. All wear the recently introduced 'Jacket, Field, M1943, Women's' and 'Trousers, Women's, Outer Cover'. The female pattern M1943 field uniform was issued to both the ANC and WAC; though it had not been available to the first nurses to land in France, it was issued soon afterwards. Well designed, warm and water-repellent, if it did not offer a perfect fit then it was certainly better than the male clothing previously issued.

(Inset E1a) First worn by US hospital stewards in 1851, the caduceus device was adopted by the US Army Medical Department in 1902. All medical personnel wore the device in its basic form, but specialist officers and civilians wore a designatory letter superimposed: 'A' for the Medical Administrative Corps, 'C' for Contract Surgeon, 'D' for Dental Corps, 'N' – as illustrated – for Army Nurse Corps, 'P' for Pharmacy Corps, 'S' for Sanitary Corps Reserve, and 'V' for Veterinary Corps.

E2: 'Gray Lady', American Red Cross Hospital & Recreation Service; USA, 1944

For walking-out volunteers of the ARC wore a smart blue-grey uniform with a cloth visored cap bearing the red cross device; in inclement weather a wool overcoat was used; both tunic and overcoat had bronze buttons with the ARC insignia. The volunteers' particular service was identified by the colour of the epaulettes; that of the Hospital & Recreation Service was grey, which along with the colour of the ward dress led

Two US ANC nurses board a transport ship encumbered with their field kit including respirators, M1936 musette packs and M1 steel helmets. Both sisters wear the OD wool 'battle' or 'Ike' jacket authorised for use in the ETO by the theatre commander. A standardised pattern for the WAC and ANC was authorised toward the end of the war, but did not see issue before VE-Day.

to the affectionate title of 'Gray Ladies'. This volunteer wears the indoor or ward dress and cap with red cross insignia, and an enamelled ARC badge pinned above the left breast pocket. Note the unusually broad white epaulettes with two buttons, one at the pointed outer end. This volunteer would have been employed in the general care and welfare of patients, including writing and reading mail, serving food and refreshment and assisting during recreation periods.

E3: Hospital Aide, Woman's Army Corps; USA, 1945
From the spring of 1943 members of the WAC and WAVES served in military hospitals; those with medical training were employed in providing basic nursing care or other medical work (although they were not a part of the nursing services), while others provided administrative support. From the first appointment of WAC hospital aides no specialist uniform had been approved; the seersucker workdress was used, but it was considered insanitary for hospital use as it also doubled as a general work dress for fatigues. The situation was temporarily relieved by the issue of the old-style nurse's blue crepe dress, which had been replaced for nurses by the wrap-over 'Uniform, Cotton, Seersucker, Nurse's'. Stocks were limited and were later supplemented by WAC cook's

whites, but neither garment provided a suitable solution. Just before the end of hostilities in Europe the OQMG eventually authorised a specialised garment, illustrated here. The beige chambray 'Dress WAC, Hospital' was a practical and attractive garment, with a full length buttoned front, two hip and one left breast pockets. The authorised issue scale of nine dresses per WAC allowed for frequent laundering. In accordance with regulations the enlisted ranks wore 'U.S.' and Medical Corps insignia on brass discs on the right and left collar points respectively.

F: UNITED STATES & CANADA
F1: Lieutenant (Junior Grade), US Navy Nurse Corps; 12th Base Hospital, Netley, England, March 1944
In June 1944 the US Navy had over 3,500 hospital beds available in the UK. The 12th Base Hospital (SNAG 56) was co-located with the US Army 110th Station Hospital. They served as transit hospitals following D-Day; wounded troops would arrive from the Continent but would stay only a short time before being moved on to other general hospitals throughout the UK. On D+4 a peak of 1,439 wounded arrived at the nearby port of Southampton, many of whom would clear through Netley. During June 1944 a total of 27,392 wounded were evacuated from France across the English Channel, 6,469 by air and 20,923 by sea; the following month the figure had risen to a total of 37,685 evacuations, 18,195 by sea and a staggering 19,959 by air.

This lieutenant j.g., one of 98 Navy nurses stationed at Netley, wears the winter outdoor uniform introduced in 1942, resembling that of the WAVES but with gold rank lace, pointed (instead of rounded) upper collar, and the special visorless cap with a gold chinstrap, with the NNC device worn on the cap crown and collar points. The uniform was modified in the summer of 1944, as described above in the body text. This Chief Nurse wears the ribbons of the American Defense and American Campaign medals; as a new arrival in theatre she has not yet been awarded the ETO ribbon.

(Inset F1a) The NNC insignia, worn both as a cap badge and as collar insignia in facing pairs, before the granting of full commissioned rank in February 1944. Thereafter it was displayed, without the 'NNC' lettering, as a cuff insignia or shirt collar device, in the same way as other USN line and staff emblems.

F2: Sister, Royal Canadian Navy; RCN Hospital Avalon, Newfoundland, 1943
Service dress for Canadian military nurses was of this same basic design for all three armed services: a mid-blue gabardine lancer-front tunic with a handkerchief displayed in the off-set right breast pocket, a matching skirt and a white veil, the parent service being identified by rank insignia and waistbelt. On the ward a white apron was worn over the uniform by nursing sisters only, senior ranks not requiring them. For walking-out a navy blue felt hat with the parent service cap insignia was worn with a 'Norfolk'-cut uniform in navy blue. This nursing sister is identified by the RCN sub-lieutenant's rank lace on naval shoulderboards; her Army counterparts wore rank 'pips', and RCAF nurses the rank lace of that service.

Although less than 350 strong, the small naval nursing branch gave distinguished service mainly in the ports at the

Canadian end of the busy and hard-fought convoy routes across the North Atlantic.

F3: Sister, Royal Canadian Army Medical Corps; No.5 Canadian Casualty Clearing Station, Liri Valley, Italy, spring 1944

Canadian nurses served in North Africa before moving on to Sicily and Italy with the advancing 8th Army. The climate saw them adopt a KD uniform better suited to field work than the normal ward uniform. This tired nursing sister, taking a break during the bloody fighting following the break-through at Cassino, wears a khaki 'aertex' shirt with the two embroidered rank 'pips' of lieutenant on epaulette slides, KD slacks, khaki veil, and the RCAMC nurse's brown leather belt with bi-metal clasp. This uniform was by no means standard; during the Liri Valley fighting nurses from Nos.4 and 5 CCSs and No.1 Canadian General Hospital served together, wearing a mix of wool or KD skirts and slacks with KD bush jackets and cotton or aertex shirts. Headwear was equally variable, including veils, headscarfs and khaki berets.

The 1943 regulations for RCAMC nurses listed the following uniform items:
Service dress (ward) Headress, tunic, skirt, belt, collar, cuffs, veil, shoes, stockings, gloves, apron.
Service suit (outdoor) Coat, skirt, shirtwaist, tie, hat, shoes, stockings, gloves, greatcoat, raincoat, scarf, cape, sweater.

Uniform items issued to RCAF and RCN nurses would have been similar to this listing. Clearly, no mention was made in regulations of the unapproved field uniform expedients.

G: AUSTRALIA, NEW ZEALAND & INDIA

G1: Sister, Australian Army Nursing Service; general hospital, New Guinea, 1943

The particularly harsh conditions encountered in New Guinea in 1942 were suffered by nurses of necessity still wearing the grey ward dress. This unacceptable situation lasted for some time; as a stop-gap an issue of male tropical clothing was made, later replaced by equally unflattering KD tunic and slacks, or a one-piece KD coverall (illustrated) together with a 'Hat, Fur Felt' (bush hat). The woman's bush hat differed from that issued to Diggers in having no provision for the brim to be fastened up, and the brim itself was proportionately wider. To identify the nurses' branch of service the drill coverall had red epaulettes with bronze rank 'pips', and a curved bronze title 'AUSTRALIA' at the base. Male pattern Jungle Green uniform saw limited use in the SW Pacific area, as did a small amount of US kit, mainly in the forward CCSs. The proximity of the front line made the carriage of steel helmets a wise precaution. A number of Australian nurses were brutally raped and murdered by Japanese troops during the opening stages of the war in the Far East.

G2: Sister, New Zealand Nursing Service; No.1 NZ Casualty Clearing Station, Western Desert, 1942

Sisters of the NZNS fared no better than the other Allies in the matter of field dress; Kiwi nurses serving in the heat and dust of the Libyan desert found themselves wearing a regulation grey ward dress, uncomfortable and difficult to launder. This sister wears the lancer-fronted dress, fastening down the left side, with an integral two-button belt; the white collar and cuffs soiled readily, so were detachable and provided in additional quantities for each dress. Corps colours were represented by the scarlet epaulettes, here bearing the usual

US Persian Gulf Service Command nurses wear a mix of OD service dress skirt and shirt, and beige 'off-duty' dress – note maroon epaulette piping and cuff braid.

two rank 'pips' of a nursing sister in bright gilt; no national title was worn. She carries an enamel basin in which she will try to wash her clothing as best she can, to maintain the high standard of hygiene demanded despite the severe shortage of water for all necessities.

Clothing regulations issued in November 1940 listed the standard NZNS uniform as comprising the following items: Coat and skirt (outdoor dress), greatcoat, dress, cape, 3 blouses, tie, shoes, stockings, hats (winter and summer), gloves, badges, overalls (ward dress), cap (veil), corridor cape. This list was supplemented by tropical uniform as required. Nurses proceeding overseas were requested to provide themselves with the following additional items: cabin trunk, holdall, small suitcase, cushion, rug, pair of galoshes, torch and batteries, looking glass, knife, fork & spoon set, 2 pairs scissors, 2 pairs forceps, 2 clinical thermometers, warm clothing as required.

G3: Sister, Indian Military Nursing Service; field hospital, Burma, 1944

In 1926 the Indian Troops Nursing Service was formed to care for native troops, who had previously been cared for at regimental level while British troops had been cared for by nurses of the QAIMNS. The ITNS was later renamed the Indian Military Nursing Service. This European IMNS sister wears the later version of the Indian grey ward dress, buttoning from right to left but with a left-to-right buttoned integral belt section. It differs from the British style in having evenly spaced black buttons down the full-length front, and a tuck/pleat at the front of each shoulder. Both long- and short-sleeved variants were used, the former having red cuffs. A similar dress in white starched cotton was also issued. The deeply pointed collar bears the IMNS insignia of a silver wreathed cross on each point; two gilt rank 'pips' are worn on the red epaulettes above the title 'IMNS'. The head veil is of the same pattern as worn by the QAIMNS.

Shortly after the first US Navy nurses arrived in England a reception was held for them at a Red Cross club. Amongst those present was the Matron-in-Chief of the QARNNS, Mrs Beale (third from left), and Mrs Baker, a QARNNS Matron (second from left), wearing 1942 navy blue 'outdoor' uniform; note the versions of the QARNNS 'tippet' rank badge worn on epaulettes and hats. The British women are seen in conversation with NNC Ensigns Teresa Mussulino and Maria Laudenscauger, wearing winter service dress complete with the distinctive visorless cap (see Plate F1).

In 1944, 250 British VAD nursing members were sent to India under the patronage of the Indian government, to assist in Indian military hospitals and to form a trained nucleus for local enrolment. VAD members serving in the Indian unit wore standard VAD uniform but were identified as being in Indian service by the use of a pair of enamelled Tudor roses on the collar points of their service dress jacket.

H: USSR, FRANCE & BELGIUM
H1: Red Army Doctor 3rd Class; Russia, 1941
Caught up in the retreats of summer 1941, this doctor wears the 'everyday' order of dress prescribed for 'commanders' of various grades – i.e. officers: the khaki male pattern M1935 *gymnastiorka* shirt-tunic with fall collar (complete with detachable white collar liner), fly front and patch breast pockets, the collar and cuffs piped red for officers; the dark blue skirt equivalent to the dark blue *sharovary* breeches of male uniform; black leather knee boots, and the brown leather 'Sam Browne' (*partupey*) M1935 belt with brass cut-out star buckle and single shoulder strap worn by officers when 'in formation'. The blue skirt was officially relegated to formal wear following the introduction of a khaki everyday skirt in 1942, although both types tended to be worn as available – as did male pattern trousers, when in the field. She wears the standard pattern khaki *pilotka* field cap, with the all-ranks red-enamelled brass star badge bearing a hammer-and-sickle motif. In August 1941 a dark blue beret was introduced exclusively for female personnel in everyday and parade orders of dress; this was supplemented in 1942 by a khaki beret for field use, the blue type then being reserved for formal wear (though both it and the khaki *pilotka* also continued in everyday use). Her branch of service is identified by M1935 collar patches (inset H1a) in dark green with red piping, and the chalice and serpent medical insignia introduced on 19 August 1924 – prior to this no badge had been worn by the medical services. The single red-enamelled bar marks the rank as equivalent to captain.

She carries a small leather double-sided case with a red cross on a small white enamel cartouche on the flap; one side was the normal despatch case, the other accom-modated a field surgical kit. Note that in this case her brassard has the red cross on a white square on a light khaki armband.

The re-introduction of *pogoni* (shoulderboards) by *Prikaz* No.25 of 15 January 1943 saw the issue of silver lace parade boards 6cm wide with green rank stripes and red edge piping for medical officers trained by the military; shoulderboards only 4cm wide were worn by doctors taken into military service but who had not graduated from military medical school. Both patterns of board bore the chalice and serpent branch badge. The 'everyday' and 'field' quality boards were khaki with the same stripes and piping and with bright and subdued rank and branch insignia respectively.

The service dress of women medical orderlies was as described above for the pre- and post-1943 periods, with appropriate insignia of rank. In the field they usually wore the full range of male combat clothing; and carried a large olive-khaki cloth medical haversack on a broad sling, its flap secured by a broad central buckled strap and marked with the red cross on a white disc.

H2: Adjudant, nursing section, Corps des Voluntaires Françaises, Forces Françaises Libres; London, 1942
The first 100 women volunteers for the Free French Forces in England, led by Lt.Simone Mathieu, were trained by the British ATS in November 1940–January 1941. In December 1941, now commanded by Lt.Hélène Terré, the unit was officially named Corps des Voluntaires Françaises, CVF (though this was also often interpreted as 'Corps des Voluntaires Féminines'). In June 1942 the unit was redes-ignated as a battalion incorporating nine sections with total strength of nine officers, 40 NCOs and 251 volunteers. Enlistees joined for the duration of the war plus three months, to serve under military discipline and wherever required. The CVF included army, navy and air force sections, and a 'social assistance' (welfare) branch which incorporated a nursing section; a detachment of the latter were shipped out to Beirut to serve with the Free French Forces in the Levant.

The uniform was that of the ATS, but by 1942 distinctive insignia had appeared. This warrant officer of the nursing section wears ATS officer's austerity pattern Service Dress,

Coffee and cookies are served up to WAVES, who have just given blood at a mobile American Red Cross clinic, by a 'Gray Lady' of the ARC Hospital & Recreation Service wearing 'indoor' or ward dress (see Plate E2).

Having escaped from France at the time of Dunkirk, these Belgian nursing officers were among five serving at a hospital in the Western Command area of Great Britain. The seated doctor is shown by her medal ribbons to be a veteran of the Great War; the nursing sister wears khaki service dress (see Plate H3).

buttoning in male fashion, her rank marked by a silver-on-black braid shoulder loop with a narrow red centre stripe. The dark blue French *bonnet de police* with a pale blue top fold seems to have been particular to the welfare and nursing sections, the others wearing a khaki and pale blue French equivalent, or the British FS cap. The original photo of this warrant officer class 2 does not feature either the brass CVF cap badge, which was a wreathed version of the collar patch motif illustrated; or rank braid at the front of the cap. National shoulder titles were seen in either black on pale blue as here, or white on black. The wreathed sword 'wings' badge of the FFL **(inset H2a)** was worn on the right breast by all ranks. The collar patches were pale blue, with the FFL motif of a sword behind a voided shield bearing the cross of Lorraine, in silver or dark blue thread. Nurses wore a red cross on a pale blue square sewn to the left upper sleeve. Like all Allied personnel in Britain she carries a service gasmask at all times.

Prior to 1943 other Frenchwomen served with volunteer FFL units in the Middle East, notably the mixed nationality field ambulance organised by Ladies Hadfield and Spears, which served in the Western Desert; and the welfare services organised in the Levant by 'La Générale' Catroux. After the garrison of French North Africa joined the Allies at the end of 1942, local recruitment brought many more Frenchwomen into a motley range of uniforms. An ambulance unit with women drivers and nurses was formed, initially from French Red Cross personnel, and attached administratively to the 27e Train, a commissariat unit. By July 1943 the complex task of organising the newly reunified French forces was sufficiently advanced for the recruitment of many volunteer nurses and other women in specialist medical categories into the army's Service de Santé, in whose units they served with the French Expeditionary Corps in Italy and later with the 1st French Army in France and Germany. (After Paul Gaujac, 'Femmes Françaises sous l'Uniforme 1940–43', *Militaria* No.161)

H3: Sister, Belgian Army; England, 1940

Following the capitulation of Belgium in May 1940, Belgian refugees were organised into the BFGB (Belgian Forces in Great Britain). Nurses from Belgium, Belgian nationals in Britain, and nurses from the unoccupied Belgian Congo rallied to the cause. Although of very limited numbers, the Belgian Army nurses provided staff for a Belgian field hospital which served in Ethiopia, Somalia and Madagascar before moving to the Far East, where the hospital was active in Burma. This nurse typically wears British ATS officer's Service Dress with Sam Browne waistbelt, and a felt hat. Gilt military buttons bear the Belgian rampant lion insignia, while the gilt wreathed cross collar insignia identify the nursing service. Interestingly, no badges of rank are worn.

INDEX

FIND OUT MORE ABOUT OSPREY

❏ Please send me the latest listing of Osprey's publications

❏ I would like to subscribe to Osprey's e-mail newsletter

Title/rank

Name

Address

Postcode/zip   state/country

e-mail

I am interested in:

❏ Ancient world
❏ Medieval world
❏ 16th century
❏ 17th century
❏ 18th century
❏ Napoleonic
❏ 19th century

❏ American Civil War
❏ World War I
❏ World War II
❏ Modern warfare
❏ Military aviation
❏ Naval warfare

Please send to:

USA & Canada:
Osprey Direct USA, c/o MBI Publishing, P.O. Box 1,
729 Prospect Avenue, Osceola, WI 54020

UK, Europe and rest of world:
Osprey Direct UK, P.O. Box 140, Wellingborough,
Northants, NN8 2FA, United Kingdom

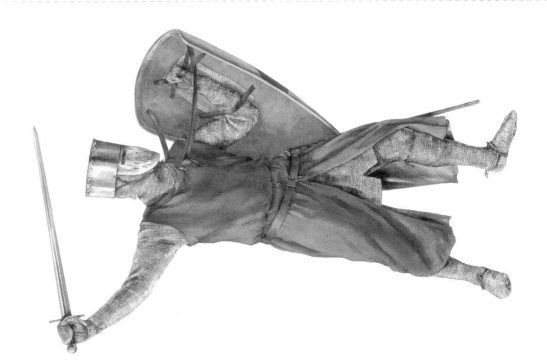

OSPREY
PUBLISHING

www.ospreypublishing.com

call our telephone hotline
for a free information pack

USA & Canada: 1-800-826-6600
UK, Europe and rest of world call:
+44 (0)1933 443 863

Young Guardsman
Figure taken from *Warrior 22:*
Imperial Guardsman 1799–1815
Published by Osprey
Illustrated by Richard Hook

Knight, c.1190
Figure taken from *Warrior 1: Norman Knight 950 – 1204 AD*
Published by Osprey
Illustrated by Christa Hook

POSTCARD